Exerci ...pany

The
Brief Holt
Handbook

Third Edition

Kirszner & Mandell

Harcourt College Publishers

Where Learning Comes to Life

TECHNOLOGY

Technology is changing the learning experience, by increasing the power of your textbook and other learning materials; by allowing you to access more information, more quickly; and by bringing a wider array of choices in your course and content information sources.

Harcourt College Publishers has developed the most comprehensive Web sites, e-books, and electronic learning materials on the market to help you use technology to achieve your goals.

PARTNERS IN LEARNING

Harcourt partners with other companies to make technology work for you and to supply the learning resources you want and need. More importantly, Harcourt and its partners provide avenues to help you reduce your research time of numerous information sources.

Harcourt College Publishers and its partners offer increased opportunities to enhance your learning resources and address your learning style. With quick access to chapter-specific Web sites and e-books . . . from interactive study materials to quizzing, testing, and career advice . . . Harcourt and its partners bring learning to life.

Harcourt's partnership with Digital:Convergence™ brings :CRQ™ technology and the :CueCat™ reader to you and allows Harcourt to provide you with a complete and dynamic list of resources designed to help you achieve your learning goals. Just swipe the cue to view a list of Harcourt's partners and Harcourt's print and electronic learning solutions.

http://www.harcourtcollege.com/partners/

Exercises to accompany

The
Brief Holt
Handbook

Third Edition

Kirszner & Mandell

Prepared by

Scott Douglass
Chattanooga State Technical Community College

Harcourt College Publishers

Fort Worth   Philadelphia   San Diego   New York   Orlando   Austin   San Antonio
Toronto   Montreal   London   Sydney   Tokyo

ISBN: 0-15-506738-9

Address for Domestic Orders
Harcourt College Publishers, 6277 Sea Harbor Drive, Orlando,
FL 32887-6777
800-782-4479

Address for International Orders
International Customer Service
Harcourt, Inc., 6277 Sea Harbor Drive, Orlando, FL 32887-6777
407-345-3800
(fax) 407-345-4060
(e-mail) hbintl@harcourt.com

Address for Editorial Correspondence
Harcourt College Publishers, 301 Commerce Street, Suite 3700,
Fort Worth, TX 76102

Web Site Address
http://www.harcourtcollege.com

Printed in the United States of America

1 2 3 4 5 6 7 8 9   202   9 8 7 6 5 4 3 2

Harcourt College Publishers

Contents

Chapter 1   Exercise A
Getting Started

Consider a book that you have recently enjoyed reading.

1. How would each of the following writing situations affect the content, style, organization, tone, and emphasis of an essay about this book?

    • A journal entry recording your informal impressions of the book

    • An examination question that asks you to summarize the book's main idea

    • A book review for a composition class in which you evaluate both the book's strengths and its weaknesses

    • A letter to your local school board in which you try to convince your readers that, regardless of the book's style or content, it should not be banned from the local public elementary schools

    • An editorial for your school newspaper in which you try to persuade other students that the book is not worth reading

2. Choose one of the writing situations listed in number 1. On a separate sheet of paper, write an opening paragraph for the specified assignment.

Chapter 1   Exercise B
Determining Your Purpose

Consider an essay subject you have chosen or your instructor has assigned. How will your purpose and audience affect what you write and how your write?

1. Name your subject.

_____

2. What is your purpose?

_____

_____

3. Who is your audience?

_____

4. What will you write and how will you write?

_____

_____

5. On a separate sheet of paper, write your first paragraph.

Chapter 1   Exercise C
Listing

Consider the variety of sources (such as people, books, magazines, observations, and so on) you encounter in a single day—sources that could provide you with useful information for the essay you are writing. In the space below, list ten of these potential sources.

1. _____

2. _____

3. _____

4. _____

5. _____

6. _____

7. _____

8. _____

9. _____

10. _____

Chapter 1   Exercise D
Freewriting

Begin with the most important sentence or idea in the paragraph you wrote in Exercise B, number 5. Freewrite until you have filled this page. If you wish, continue to freewrite on a separate sheet of paper.

_____

_____

_____

_____

_____

_____

_____

_____

_____

Harcourt, Inc.

Name _____ Date _____ Score _____

Chapter 1   Exercise E
Brainstorming

Consider what you have discovered in Exercises B, C, and D. Do you need to change any part of your plan for your essay?

1. Name your subject.

_____

2. What is your purpose?

_____

_____

3. Who is your audience?

_____

4. List all the points you can think of that seem pertinent to your essay.

_____

_____

_____

Name _____ Date _____ Score _____

Chapter 1   Exercise F
Journal Entry

Write a journal entry evaluating your progress so far. Which of the strategies for finding something to write worked best for you? Why?

_____

_____

_____

_____

_____

_____

_____

_____

_____

Harcourt, Inc.

Chapter 1   Exercise G
Cluster Diagram / Topic Tree

Review the work you did for Exercises B-F. Use this material to help
you construct a cluster diagram or a topic tree. This exercise should
help you to see how the ideas you have discovered can be organized
into related groups.

_____

_____

_____

_____

_____

_____

_____

_____

_____

Chapter 1   Exercise H
Developing a Thesis

Analyze the following statements or topics, and then explain why none of them qualifies as an effective thesis. Be prepared to explain how each could be improved.

1. In this essay, I will examine the environmental effects of residential and commercial development on the coastal regions of the United States.

2. Residential and commercial development in the coastal regions of the United States

3. How to avoid coastal overdevelopment

4. Coastal development: pro and con

5. Residential and commercial development of America's coastal regions benefits some people, but it has some disadvantages.

6. The environmentalists' position on coastal development

7. More and more coastal regions in the United States are being overdeveloped.

8. Residential and commercial development guidelines need to be developed for coastal regions of the United States.

9. Coastal development is causing beach erosion.

10. At one time, I enjoyed walking on the beach, but commercial and residential development has ruined the experience for me.

Name _____ Date _____ Score _____

Chapter 1   Exercise I
Stating a Thesis

On a separate sheet of paper, formulate a clearly worded thesis statement for each of the following topics.

1. A person who has profoundly influenced the course of your life

2. Gun control and the Second Amendment

3. Should medical use of marijuana be made lawful?

4. Preparing for your retirement

5. The value of a college education

6. Public funding of the arts

7. Shoplifting

8. The role of cultural diversity

9. Parochial vs. secular education

10. Political correctness and the First Amendment

Chapter 1   Exercise J
Stating a Thesis

Review the cluster diagram or the topic tree you made in Exercise G. Use it to help you develop a thesis for an essay. Write your thesis in the space below.

_____

_____

_____

_____

_____

_____

_____

_____

_____

Harcourt, Inc.

Chapter 1   Exercise K
Informal Outline

After reviewing your notes, prepare an informal outline for a paper on
the thesis you developed in Exercise J.

_____

_____

_____

_____

_____

_____

_____

_____

_____

Chapter 1   Exercise L
Rough Draft

Write a rough draft of the essay you have been planning. In the space provided, begin your rough draft. Then use your own paper to complete the rough draft.

_____

_____

_____

_____

_____

_____

_____

_____

_____

Chapter 1   Exercise M
Collaborative Revision

After you have drafted a paper, form teams of two or three for collaborative revision. Read each other's papers and write responses to the "Questions for Collaborative Revision" below. Then discuss the comments.

- What is the essay about? Is the topic suitable for this assignment?

- What is the main point of the essay? Is the thesis stated? If so, is it clearly worded? If not, how can the wording be improved? Is the thesis stated in an appropriate location?

- Is the essay arranged logically? Do the body paragraphs appear in an appropriate order?

- What ideas support the thesis? Does each body paragraph develop one of these?

- Does each body paragraph have a unifying idea? Are topic sentences needed to summarize the information in the paragraphs? Are the topic sentences clearly related to the thesis?

- Is any necessary information missing? Identify any areas that seem to need further development. Is any information irrelevant? If so, indicate possible deletions.

- Can you contribute anything to the essay? Can you offer any ideas or examples from your own reading, experience, or observations that would strengthen the writer's points?

- Can you follow the writer's ideas? If not, would clearer connections between sentences or paragraphs be helpful? If so, where are such connections needed?

- Is the introductory paragraph interesting to you? Would another kind of introduction work better?

- Does the conclusion leave you with a sense of completion? Would another kind of conclusion be more appropriate?

- Is anything unclear or confusing?

- What is the essay's chief strength? What is its chief weakness?

Name _____ Date _____ Score _____

Chapter 1   Exercise N
Customized Checklist

Using the revision checklists on pages 24-26 of *The* Brief *Holt Handbook* as a guide, create a "customized checklist"—one that reflects the specific concerns that are <u>most</u> <u>important</u> <u>to</u> <u>you</u> as you revise your essay. Then revise your essay according to this checklist. Use your own paper as necessary.

_____

_____

_____

_____

_____

_____

_____

_____

After you have completed this revision, edit your essay and then prepare a final draft, being sure to proofread it carefully.

Chapter 1   Exercise O
Central Idea—Topic Sentence

The following paragraph is unified by a central idea, but that idea is not explicitly stated. After you have read the entire paragraph, identify the paragraph's unifying idea, write a topic sentence that expresses it, and indicate with a caret (^) where the topic sentence should be placed in the paragraph.

"Lite" can mean a product has fewer calories, or less fat, or less sodium, or it can simply mean the product has a "light" color, texture, or taste. It may mean none of these. Food can be advertised as 86 percent fat free when it is actually 50 percent fat. This "confusion" is considered acceptable because the term "fat free" is based on weight, and fat is extremely light. Another misleading term is "no cholesterol," which is found on some products that never had any cholesterol in the first place. Peanut butter, for example, contains no cholesterol—a fact that manufacturers have recently made an issue—but it is very high in fat and so would not be a very good food for most dieters. Sodium labeling presents still another problem. The terms "sodium free," "very low sodium," "low sodium," "reduced sodium," and "no salt added" have very specific meanings, frequently not explained on the packages on which they appear.

_____

_____

_____

Chapter 1   Exercise P
Central Idea—Topic Sentence

The following paragraph is unified by a central idea, but that idea is not explicitly stated. After you have read the entire paragraph, identify the paragraph's unifying idea, write a topic sentence that expresses it, and indicate with a caret (^) where the topic sentence should be placed in the paragraph.

The narrator in Ellison's novel leaves an all-black college in the South to seek his fortune—and his identity—in the North. Throughout the story, he experiences bigotry in a variety of forms. Blacks as well as whites, friends as well as enemies, treat him according to their preconceived notions of what he should be, or how he can help to advance their causes. Clearly, this is a book about racial prejudice. However, on another level, *Invisible Man* is more than the account of a young African-American's initiation into the harsh realities of life in the United States before the civil rights movement. The narrator calls himself invisible because others refuse to see him. He becomes so alienated from society—black and white—that he chooses to live in isolation. But, when he has learned to see himself clearly, he will emerge demanding that others see him, too.

_____

_____

_____

_____

Harcourt, Inc.

Chapter 2   Exercise A
Coherence within Paragraphs

Read the following paragraph and determine how the author achieves coherence. Underline parallel elements, pronouns, repeated words, and transitional words and phrases that link sentences. Label these devices in the margins.

Some years ago, the old elevated railway in Philadelphia was torn down and replaced by the subway system. This ancient El with its barnlike stations containing nut-vending machines and scattered food scraps had, for generations, been the favorite feeding ground of flocks of pigeons, generally one flock to a station along the route of the El. Hundreds of pigeons were dependent upon the system. They flapped in and out of its stanchions and steel work or gathered in watchful little audiences about the feet of anyone who rattled the peanut-vending machines. They even watched people who jingled change in their hands, and prospected for food under the feet of the crowds who gathered between trains. Probably very few among the waiting people who tossed a crumb to an eager pigeon realized that this El was like a food-bearing river, and that the life which haunted its banks was dependent upon the running of the trains with their human freight.

(Loren Eiseley, *The Night Country*)

Chapter 2   Exercise B
Coherence within Paragraphs

Insert missing transitional words and phrases to revise the following paragraph and make it coherent. Write your changes between the lines.

The theory of continental drift was first put forward by Alfred Wegener in 1912. The continents fit together like a gigantic jigsaw puzzle. The opposing Atlantic coasts, especially South America and Africa, seem to have been attached. He believed that at one time, probably 225 million years ago, there was one supercontinent. This continent broke into parts that drifted into their present positions. The theory stirred controversy during the 1920s and eventually was ridiculed by the scientific community. In 1954, the theory was revived. The theory of continental drift is now accepted as a reasonable geological explanation of the continental system.

Chapter 2   Exercise C
Coherence among Paragraphs

Read the following paragraph cluster. Then, on your own paper, rewrite the paragraphs and revise as necessary to increase coherence among them.

Leave It to Beaver and *Father Knows Best* were typical of the late 1950s and early 1960s. Both were popular during a time when middle-class mothers stayed home to raise their children while fathers went to "the office." The Beaver's mother, June Cleaver, always wore a dress and high heels, even when she vacuumed. So did Margaret Anderson, the mother on *Father Knows Best*. Wally and the Beaver lived a picture-perfect small-town life, and Betty, Bud, and Kathy never had a problem that father Jim Anderson couldn't solve.

The Brady Bunch featured six children and the typical Mom-at-home and Dad-at-work combination. Of course, Florence Brady did wear pants, and the Bradys were what today would be called a "blended family." Nevertheless, *The Brady Bunch* presented a hopelessly idealized picture of upper-middle-class suburban life. The Brady kids lived in a large split-level house, went on vacations, had two loving parents, and even had a live-in maid, the ever-faithful, wisecracking Alice. Everyone in town was heterosexual, employed, able-bodied, and white.

The Cosby Show was extremely popular. It featured two professional parents—a doctor and a lawyer. They lived in a townhouse with original art on the walls, and money never seemed to be a problem. In addition to warm relationships with their siblings, the Huxtable children also had close ties to their grandparents. *The Cosby Show* did introduce problems, such as so Theo's dyslexia, but in many ways it replicated the 1950s formula. Even in the 1990s, it seems father still knew best.

Chapter 2   Exercise D
Patterns of Paragraph Development

Determine one possible method of development for a paragraph on each of these topics. Then, on a separate sheet of paper, write a paragraph on one of the topics.

1. Depending on friends for transportation

2. An unexpected bill for automobile repairs

3. A perfect spot to take a vacation

4. Troubles that accompany being computer illiterate

5. The ideal campsite

6. The most useful software titles

7. The perils of not backing up computer files

8. The benefits of extracurricular activities

9. Jobs to avoid

10. The types of people who go to concerts

Harcourt, Inc.

Chapter 2   Exercise E
Well-Developed Paragraphs

Read the following paragraph and then answer these questions.

1.   In general terms, how could the paragraph be developed further?

2.   What pattern of development might be used?

    Civility once was considered the cornerstone of a progressive society. Disagreements were noted, but seldom publicly acknowledged. Violation of this custom among certain classes often resulted in the practice of dueling, which acted as a deterrent to uncivil behavior because of the finality of the outcome. Although dueling is now outlawed in our society, many disagreements are still settled through violence. The lack of civility remains problematic in our society.

Chapter 2   Exercise F
Well-Developed Paragraphs

Read the following paragraph and then answer these questions.

1. In general terms, how could the paragraph be developed further?

2. What pattern of development might be used?

Amish Friendship Bread is a culinary treat. It begins with the receipt of a gift of a batch of starter batter. The entire process—from receiving the batter to the finished product—takes ten days. The first day requires the addition of flour, milk, and sugar. Days two through five involve the once-a-day, gentle mixing of the batter. On day six, more milk, flour, and sugar are added. Days seven through nine repeat the daily mixing. On day ten, the long-anticipated outcome is realized as a portion of the batter is baked into a succulent loaf, while saving a starter batch to share with a friend.

Harcourt, Inc.

Review Exercise A for Chapters 1-2
Writing Essays and Paragraphs

In the space provided, add further development to the ideas presented in the following paragraph. If you need additional space, complete the assignment on your own paper.

Most people look forward to vacations with great eagerness. Where they vacation, however, differs widely. Vacation locations depend on such factors as personal preference, financial considerations, and time available. Some people look forward to spending a few days in the mountains, while others can think of nothing more pleasant than sunning on a sugar-white beach. Regardless of their choices, vacations remain the goal and basis of fond memories for nearly everyone.

_____

_____

_____

_____

_____

_____

_____

Review Exercise B for Chapters 1-2
Writing Essays and Paragraphs

In the space provided, add further development to the ideas presented in the following paragraph. If you need additional space, complete the assignment on your own paper.

Young adults are social creatures. They enjoy gathering with others their age to celebrate various types of occasions. For example, an overnight tailgate party may precede a football game, or a group may gather for a clambake on a beach, or spring break may demand a special celebration. No matter the type of gathering, attention must be paid to details in order to make the celebration memorable.

_____

_____

_____

_____

_____

_____

_____

_____

Harcourt, Inc.

Chapter 3   Exercise A
Thinking Critically

Some of the following statements are facts; others are opinions. Identify each fact with the letter *F* and each opinion with the letter *O*. Then consider what kind of evidence, if any, could support each opinion.

1. The Charles River and Boston Harbor currently test much lower for common pollutants than they did ten years ago.

2. We no longer need to worry about environmental legislation because we've made great advances in cleaning up our environment.

3. The television rating system uses a system similar to the familiar movie rating codes to let parents know how appropriate a certain show might be for their children.

4. The new television rating system would be better if it gave specifics about the violence, sexual innuendo, and language content in rated television programs.

Chapter 3   Exercise B
Thinking Critically

Some of the following statements are facts; others are opinions. Identify each fact with the letter *F* and each opinion with the letter *O*. Then consider what kind of evidence, if any, could support each opinion.

1. The incidence of violent crime fell in the first six months of 1996.

2. New gun laws and more police officers led to a decrease in crime in 1996.

3. Affirmative action laws and policies have helped women and minority group members advance in the workplace.

4. Affirmative action policies have outlived their usefulness.

5. Women who work are better off today than they were twenty years ago.

6. The wage gap between men and women in similar jobs is smaller now than it was twenty years ago.

Harcourt, Inc.

Chapter 4   Exercise A
Writing Argumentative Essays

For each of the following statements, list three arguments in favor and three arguments against.

1. Colleges and universities should provide free child care for children of currently enrolled students.

For _____

_____

_____

Against _____

_____

_____

2. Public school students should have to wear school uniforms.

For _____

_____

_____

Against _____

_____

_____

Chapter 4   Exercise B
Writing Argumentative Essays

For each of the following statements, list three arguments in favor and three arguments against.

1. Retirees earning more than $50,000 a year should not be eligible for Social Security benefits.

For _____

_____

_____

Against _____

_____

_____

2. The federal government should limit the amount of violence shown on television.

For _____

_____

_____

Against _____

_____

_____

Review Exercise A for Chapters 3-4
Critical Thinking and Argumentation

1. Read the following student paragraph and evaluate its supporting evidence.

The United States is becoming more and more violent every day. I was talking to my friend Debbie, and she mentioned that a guy her roommate knows was attacked at dusk and had his skull crushed by the barrel of a gun. Later, she heard that he was in the hospital with a blood clot in his brain. Two friends of mine were walking home from a party when they were attacked by armed men right outside the A-Plus Mini Market. These two examples make it very clear to me how violent our nation is becoming. My art professor, who is in his fifties, remembers a few similar violent incidents occurring when he was growing up, and he was even mugged in London last year. He believes that if London police carried guns, the city would be safer. Two of the twenty-five people in our class have been the victims of violent crime, and I feel lucky that I am not one of them.

Review Exercise A for Chapters 3-4 (continued)
Critical Thinking and Argumentation

2. In the space below, create your own version of an argument based on insufficient supporting evidence. As the topic for this paragraph, take a stance regarding the role that television has played in the pattern of declining scores on reading comprehension tests during the past twenty-five years.

_____

_____

_____

_____

_____

_____

_____

_____

_____

Harcourt, Inc.

Review Exercise B for Chapters 3-4
Critical Thinking and Argumentation

Revise the following draft of an argumentative essay, paying particular attention to the essay's logic, its use of support, and the writer's efforts to establish credibility. Be prepared to identify the changes you made and to explain how they make the essay more convincing. If necessary, revise further to strengthen coherence, unity, and style.

Television Violence: Let Us Exercise Our Choice

Television began as what many people thought was a fad. Now, over fifty years later, it is the subject of arguments and controversy. There are even some activist groups who spend all their time protesting television's role in society. The weirdest of these groups is definitely the one that attacks television for being too violent. As far as I am concerned, these people should find better things to do with their time. There is nothing wrong with American television that a little bit of parental supervision wouldn't fix.

The best argument against these protest groups is that television gives people what they want. I am not an expert on the subject, but I do know that the broadcasting industry is a business, a very serious business. Television programming has to give people what they want, or else they won't watch it. This is a fact that many of the so-called experts forget. If the television networks followed the advice of the protestors, they would be out of business within a year.

(This essay continues on the next page.)

Review Exercise B for Chapters 3-4 (continued)
Critical Thinking and Argumentation

Another argument against the protest groups is that the First Amendment of the US Constitution guarantees all citizens the right of free speech. I am a citizen, so I should be able to watch whatever I want to. If these protestors do not want to watch violent programs, let them change the channel or turn off their sets. The Founding Fathers realized that an informed citizenry is the best defense against tyranny. Look at some of the countries that control the programs that citizens are able to watch. In Iran and in China, for example, people see only what the government wants them to see. A citizen can be put into prison if he or she is caught watching an illegal program. Is this where our country is heading?

Certainly, American society is too violent. No one can deny this fact, but we cannot blame all the problems of American society on television violence. As far as I know, there is absolutely no proof that the violence that people see on television causes them to act violently. Violence in society is probably caused by a number of things—drugs, the proliferation of guns, and increased unemployment, for example. Before focusing on violence on television, the protestors should address these things.

All things considered, the solution to violence on television is simple: parents should monitor what their children watch. If they don't like what their children are watching, they should change the channel or turn off the television. There is no reason why the majority of television watchers—who are for the most part law-abiding people—should have to stop watching programs they like. I for one do not want some protestor telling me what I can or cannot watch, and if, by chance, these protestors do succeed in eliminating all violence, the result will be television programming that is boring, and television, the vast wasteland, will suddenly be turned into the dull wasteland.

Harcourt, Inc.

Chapter 5   Exercise A
Time Management

The following schedule will not only give you an overview of the research process, but it will also help you manage your time.

Activity	*Date Due*	*Date Completed*
Choosing a Topic	_____	_____
Focusing on a Research Question	_____	_____
Doing Exploratory Research	_____	_____
Assembling a Working Bibliography and Making Bibliography Cards	_____	_____
Doing Focused Research and Taking Notes	_____	_____
Outlining	_____	_____
Drafting	_____	_____
Revising	_____	_____
Preparing a Final Draft	_____	_____

Chapter 5   **Exercise B**
Discovering Your Research Question

List five subjects you want to know more about.

1. _____

2. _____

3. _____

4. _____

5. _____

Chapter 5   Exercise C
Discovering Your Research Question

For each of the following, base your response on the list you created in Exercise B. Identify the subject by citing its corresponding number as it appears in Exercise B.

1. Which subject would be most interesting for you to do research and write about? Why?

_____ _____

_____

_____

2. Which subject would be most interesting for your audience to read about? Why?

_____ _____

_____

_____

3. Which subject would best lend itself to the assignment you have been given? How?

_____ _____

_____

Chapter 5   Exercise D
Discovering Your Research Question

For each of the following, base your response on the list you created in Exercise B. Identify the subject by citing its corresponding number as it appears in Exercise B.

1. For which of these subjects would you
    be able to locate the best source material?   _____

2. Which subject do you choose? Why?

_____ _____

_____

_____

3. In the form of a question, record what you hope to find out by
    doing research and writing about this subject.

_____

_____

_____

Chapter 6   Exercise A
Exploring Your Topic and Locating Sources

List the reference books, bibliographies, periodicals, indexes, databases, and other resources that are related to your subject and available to you. Add to this list as you make discoveries in the course of your research and writing. Be sure to record all the information you will need for documenting your sources.

_____

_____

_____

_____

_____

_____

_____

_____

_____

Chapter 6   Exercise B
Exploring Your Topic and Locating Sources

Search the resources that you identified in Exercise A. List the books, articles, people, organizations, and other material that you think will be most useful to you. Write a brief note to help you remember what you hope to learn or gain from each source. What do you expect each source to contribute to your research and paper? Revise this list as you continue to locate and evaluate source material. (Look ahead to Exercise C in this chapter and to Exercises A, B, and C in Chapter 7.) Be sure to record all information you will need for documenting your sources.

_____

_____

_____

_____

_____

_____

_____

_____

Name _____ Date _____ Score _____

Chapter 6   Exercise C
Evaluating Sources

Select one of the sources that you have identified (book, essay, or article from a newspaper, magazine, or journal), and then analyze its use of source materials.

1. What types of materials are used?

_____

_____

_____

2. Does the writer use more direct quotations than paraphrases? Are you able to determine why? If so, explain.

_____

_____

3. How does the writer give the reader a sense of the source's validity or credibility?

_____

_____

_____

Chapter 6   Exercise D
Evaluating Sources

Select another of the sources that you have identified (book, essay, or article from a newspaper, magazine, or journal), and then analyze its use of source materials. (This repeats Exercise C, but with a second source.)

1. What types of materials are used?

    _____

    _____

2. Does the writer use more direct quotations than paraphrases? Are you able to determine why? If so, explain.

    _____

    _____

3. How does the writer give the reader a sense of the source's validity or credibility?

    _____

    _____

    _____

            Harcourt, Inc.

Chapter 7   Exercise A
Locating and Evaluating Sources on the Web Using URLs

Using the Web browser that you prefer, enter a URL for one of the Selected Web Sites found on pages 128-29 in *The* Brief *Holt Handbook*. Answer the following questions. Also, print at least the first screen of the Web site.

1. Does the site include a list of Contents that tells you the general topics? If so, what are the general topics?

    _____

    _____

2. Scroll to the bottom of the home page to locate the person responsible for managing the site (often referred to as the "Webmaster"). Is a name mentioned on this site?

    _____

3. Does the site mention when it was last updated? If so, record it.

    _____

4. Click on links to browse through the site. Is navigation easy? Is the site's organization easily understood?

    _____

Chapter 7   Exercise B
Locating and Evaluating Sources on the Web
    Using a Key Word Search

Using the Web browser and search engine that you prefer, complete the
following tasks.

Type in: **Sistine Chapel**

1.   How many documents are found?   _____

2.   How are the listed documents sorted? (usually by relevance or site)

     _____

3.   Are any of the listed documents commercial?   _____
     (Are they basically advertisements for a
     publisher, textbook, tour guide, or airline?)

     _____

4.   Are any of the listed documents unrelated   _____
     to the Sistine Chapel? If so, estimate the percentage.

Name _____ Date _____ Score _____

Chapter 7   Exercise C
Doing Your Own Key Word Search

Type in your own key word search on a topic of your choosing, revising the key words as necessary to obtain a manageable list of documents. Select one document, and then respond to these questions. Print at least the first screen of the Web site you select.

1. What is the source of the information?

_____

2. Is the Webmaster identified? Do you have reason to consider this author credible and reliable? Explain.

_____

3. Does the site mention when it was last updated? If so, record it.

_____

4. Does the text adhere to the conventions of research material that would be expected from print material? If so, briefly describe how the document meets those conventions. If not, what is lacking?

_____

5. Briefly evaluate the graphics, sound, or video. Are they used to enhance the text, or do they mask a lack of solid content?

_____

Chapter 7   Exercise D
Citing Electronic Sources

Consult *The* Brief *Holt Handbook* and use proper documentation format for electronic sources to complete the following tasks.

1. Cite the source you used in **Exercise A: Locating and Evaluating Sources on the Web Using URLs**.

    _____

    _____

2. Cite one source you located in **Exercise B: Locating and Evaluating Sources on the Web Using a Key Word Search**.

    _____

    _____

3. Cite the source you used in **Exercise C: Doing Your Own Key Word Search**.

    _____

    _____

Chapter 8   Exercise A
Integrating Sources and Avoiding Plagiarism

Assume that, during your preparation for a paper on "the rise of suburbia," you encountered the following passage from the book *Great Expectations: America and the Baby Boom Generation* by Landon Y. Jones (New York: Ballantine, 1986). Read the passage and then, on your own paper, write a brief summary.

As an internal migration, the settling of the suburbs was phenomenal. In the twenty years from 1950 to 1970, the population of the suburbs doubled from 36 million to 72 million. No less than 83 percent of the total population growth in the United States during the 1950s was in the suburbs, which were growing fifteen times faster than any other segment of the country. As people packed and moved, the national mobility rate leaped by 50 percent. The only other comparable influx was the wave of European immigrants to the United States around the turn of the century. But as *Fortune* pointed out, more people moved to the suburbs every year than had ever arrived on Ellis Island.

Chapter 8   Exercise B
Integrating Sources and Avoiding Plagiarism

This is a continuation of the passage from *Great Expectations: America and the Baby Boom Generation* by Landon Y. Jones (New York: Ballantine, 1986). Read this portion and then, on your own paper, write a brief summary.

By now, bulldozers were churning up dust storms as they cleared the land for housing developments. More than a million acres of farmland were plowed under every year during the 1950s. Millions of apartment-dwelling parents with two children were suddenly realizing that two children could be doubled up in a spare bedroom, but a third child cried loudly for something more. The proportion of new houses with three or more bedrooms, in fact, rose from one-third in 1947 to three-quarters in 1954. The necessary *Lebensraum* could only be found in the suburbs. There was a housing shortage, but young couples armed with VA and FHA loans built their dream homes with easy credit and free spending habits that were unthinkable to the baby-boom grandparents, who shook their heads with the Depression still fresh in their memories. Of the 13 million homes built in the decade before 1958, 11 million of them—or 85 percent—were built in the suburbs. Home ownership rose 50 percent between 1940 and 1950, and another 50 percent by 1960. By then, one-fourth of *all* housing in the United Sates had been built in the fifties. For the first time, more Americans owned homes than rented them.

Chapter 8   Exercise C
Integrating Sources and Avoiding Plagiarism

This is a continuation of the passage from *Great Expectations: America and the Baby Boom Generation* by Landon Y. Jones (New York: Ballantine, 1986). Read this portion and then, on your own paper, write a brief summary.

We were becoming a land of gigantic nurseries. The biggest were built by Abraham Levitt, the son of poor Russian-Jewish immigrants, who had originally built houses for the Navy during the war. The first of three East Coast Levittowns went up on the potato fields of Long Island. Exactly $7900—or $60 a month and no money down—bought you a Monopoly-board bungalow with four rooms, attic, washing machine, outdoor barbecue, and a television set built into the wall. The 17,447 units eventually became home to 82,000 people, many of whom were pregnant or wanted to be. In a typical story on the suburban explosion, one magazine breathlessly described a volleyball game of nine couples in which no less than five of the women were expecting.

Chapter 8   Exercise D
Paraphrase

In the space below, **paraphrase** the paragraph printed in Exercise C.
If necessary, complete this assignment on your own paper.

_____

_____

_____

_____

_____

_____

_____

_____

_____

Chapter 8   Exercise E
Quoting

In the space below, write a paragraph for a paper on "the rise of suburbia" combining summary, paraphrase, and quotation of the excerpts from *Great Expectations* that appear in Exercises A, B, and C. Be prepared to explain why you used summary, paraphrase, and quotation as you did.

_____

_____

_____

_____

_____

_____

_____

_____

_____

Chapter 8   Exercise F
Documentation

1. Insert the necessary MLA-style parenthetical citation(s) of source material into the paragraph you wrote for Exercise E. Publication information for *Great Expectations* appears in Exercise A. Assume that the page number you need to refer to is 27.

_____

_____

_____

_____

_____

_____

2. In the space below, write the entry you would use for *Great Expectations* on your MLA-style Works Cited page.

_____

_____

Review Exercise A for Chapters 5-8
Research

In the space below, record five points with which you were familiar as you began this research unit, but which became more helpful after you had completed Exercises 5-8.

1. _____

_____

2. _____

_____

3. _____

_____

4. _____

_____

5. _____

_____

Review Exercise A for Chapters 5-8 (continued)
Research

In the space below, record five points that were entirely new to you when you began this research unit, but now (after completing Exercises 5-8) you realize that they have merit and will likely prove helpful as you complete your next research assignment.

1. _____

_____

2. _____

_____

3. _____

_____

4. _____

_____

5. _____

_____

Harcourt, Inc.

Review Exercise B for Chapters 5-8
Research

In the space below, record five points which you've found especially helpful and which you would offer as recommendations to someone new to the Internet.

1. _____

   _____

2. _____

   _____

3. _____

   _____

4. _____

   _____

5. _____

   _____

Review Exercise B for Chapters 5-8 (continued)
Research

In the space below, record five problem areas which you've encountered related to the Internet and which you would encourage others to avoid.

1. _____

_____

2. _____

_____

3. _____

_____

4. _____

_____

5. _____

_____

Harcourt, Inc.

Chapter 9   Exercise A
MLA Documentation Format

For each of the following types of sources, provide a bibliographic entry that complies with MLA documentation guidelines.

A book by two authors

_____

_____

_____

An edited book

_____

_____

_____

An article in a monthly magazine

_____

_____

_____

Chapter 9   Exercise B
MLA Documentation Format

For each of the following types of sources, provide a bibliographic entry that complies with MLA documentation guidelines.

A signed article in a newspaper

_____

_____

_____

A non-periodical publication on CD-ROM (such as Encarta®)

_____

_____

_____

A Web page

_____

_____

_____

Harcourt, Inc.

Chapter 10   Exercise A
APA and Other Documentation Formats

For each of the following types of sources, provide a bibliographic entry that complies with APA documentation guidelines.

A book by two authors

_____

_____

_____

An edited book

_____

_____

_____

An article in a monthly magazine

_____

_____

_____

A signed article in a newspaper

_____

_____

_____

Chapter 10   Exercise B
APA and Other Documentation Formats

For each of the following types of sources, provide a bibliographic entry that complies with CME documentation guidelines.

A book by two authors

_____

_____

_____

An edited book

_____

_____

_____

An article in a monthly magazine

_____

_____

_____

A signed article in a newspaper

_____

_____

_____

Review Exercise A for Chapters 9-10
Survival Skills

The following notes identify sources used in a paper on censorship and the Internet. Following the proper format for MLA documentation, create a bibliographic entry for each source.

1. An essay by Nat Hentoff entitled Speech Should Not Be Limited on pages 22-26 of the book Censorship: Opposing Viewpoints, edited by Terry O'Neill. Greenhaven Press in St. Paul, Minnesota, publishes the book. The publication year is 1985.

_____

_____

_____

2. If You Don't Love It, Leave It, an essay by Esther Dyson in the New York Times Magazine, July 15, 1995, on pages 26 and 27.

_____

_____

_____

Review Exercise B for Chapters 9-10
Survival Skills

The following notes identify sources used in a paper on censorship and the Internet. Following the proper format for MLA documentation, create a bibliographic entry for each source.

1. Terry O'Neill's introduction to Censorship: Opposing Viewpoints, found on pages 13 and 14. Greenhaven Press in St. Paul, Minnesota, publishes the book. The publication year is 1985.

_____

_____

_____

2. An essay in the Village Voice entitled The Speech Police Invade Cyberspace by Nat Hentoff. It was published on July 11, 1995, on pages 22 and 23.

_____

_____

_____

Chapter 11   Exercise A
Developing Reading Skills

Consult the Highlighting Symbols Checklist found in Chapter 11 of *The* Brief *Holt Handbook*, Select the highlighting methods that you consider most appropriate. Then highlight the following passage in a manner that would help you review it, if the need should arise.

One of the more intriguing literary legends surrounding the King James Version of the Bible alleges that Shakespeare's hand is present in the 46th Psalm. Turn to the psalm to see for yourself. Count to the forty-sixth word from the beginning of the psalm (*shake*) and then identify the forty-sixth word from the end of the psalm (*spear*). These findings might be dismissed as merely interesting coincidence. The situation becomes even more intriguing, however, when we realize that Shakespeare was forty-six years old when the revision was underway in 1610. We shouldn't be surprised to find that Shakespeare played a role in translating this magnificently poetic portion of the King James Version.

Chapter 11   Exercise B
Developing Reading Skills

Consult the Highlighting Symbols Checklist found in Chapter 11 of *The Brief Holt Handbook*, Select the highlighting methods that you consider most appropriate. Then highlight the following passage in a manner that would help you review it, if the need should arise.

Giorgio Vasari, the Italian art historian who lived during the sixteenth century, records an interesting anecdote concerning Leonardo's *The Last Supper*. For his models of the disciples, Leonardo drew from life, encountering difficulty only in locating a suitable Judas Iscariot. Throughout much of his work on the painting, Leonardo was troubled by the prior of Santa Maria, who monitored the work's progress from a vantage uncomfortably close for the artist. Upon hearing that the prior had expressed his concerns to Duke Sforza, Leonardo mentioned that any delay he had experienced was merely the result of his having encountered difficulty in identifying a model for the betrayer. But, Leonardo pointed out, he would be delayed no longer, for he had located his model: the prior would serve nicely.

Chapter 12   Exercise A
Writing Essay Examinations

Read each of the following essay examination topics and determine what kind of question it poses. Does it ask for comparison and contrast, division and classification, or cause and effect?

1. Discuss the most appealing characteristics that you find at three of your favorite campgrounds.

   _____

2. Discuss the consequences of poor preparation for a camping trip.

   _____

3. Identify the characteristics of three types of sleeping bags that you have considered owning.

   _____

4. Discuss the advantages and disadvantages of two pairs of hiking boots that you have considered purchasing.

   _____

5. Explain why you chose to hike forty-five miles of the Appalachian Trail during Spring Break, instead of accompanying your friends on their trip to Panama City Beach, Florida.

   _____

Chapter 12   Exercise B
Writing Essay Examinations

Select three of the essay examination topics found in Exercise A. For each topic, compose the topic sentence that you might use to begin your essay response.

_____

_____

_____

_____

_____

_____

_____

_____

_____

_____

Name _____ Date _____ Score _____

Chapter 13   Exercise A
Writing about Literature

Assume that your instructor has assigned an essay in which you are to provide a summary of the scholarly comments that have been written about *Hamlet* during the past ten years. Identify five credible sources that you would consider appropriate for your purposes.

1. _____

2. _____

3. _____

4. _____

5. _____

Chapter 13   Exercise B
Writing about Literature

Assume that your instructor has assigned an essay in which you are to provide a summary of the scholarly comments that have been written about *Hamlet* during the past ten years. Identify five unworthy sources that you would consider inappropriate for your purposes.

1. _____

2. _____

3. _____

4. _____

5. _____

Name _____ Date _____ Score _____

Chapter 14   Exercise A
Document Design and Manuscript Format

Assume that you are beginning the final version of your essay for submission. The area below is intended to represent the initial page of your essay. Based on the MLA Manuscript Guidelines, provide the appropriate information that would appear atop the first page, plus the title and the essay's first sentence. For your convenience, lines have been provided.

Name _____ Date _____ Score _____

Chapter 14   Exercise B
Document Design and Manuscript Format

Assume that you are preparing for submission the Works Consulted page that will serve as page 6 when it accompanies your essay. The area below is intended to represent the Works Consulted page for your essay. Based on the MLA Manuscript Guidelines, provide the appropriate information that would appear atop the Works Consulted page, plus the first three entries. For your convenience, lines have been provided.

_____

_____

_____

_____

_____

_____

_____

_____

_____

_____

_____

Chapter 15   Exercise A
Writing for the Workplace

Think of a job that you would like to have ten years after you complete your college education. In the space below, provide a letter of application in the semiblock format. Continue the letter on the back of this page.

_____

_____

_____

_____

_____

_____

_____

_____

_____

_____

Chapter 15   Exercise A (continued)
Writing for the Workplace

Continue the letter of application in the space below.

_____

_____

_____

_____

_____

_____

_____

_____

_____

_____

Chapter 15   Exercise B
Writing for the Workplace

In the space below, provide a sample résumé in chronological order to accompany the letter of application you created in Exercise A. Continue the résumé on the back of this page.

_____

_____

_____

_____

_____

_____

_____

_____

_____

_____

Chapter 15   Exercise B (continued)
Writing for the Workplace

Continue the résumé in the space below.

_____

_____

_____

_____

_____

_____

_____

_____

_____

_____

Harcourt, Inc.

Name _____ Date _____ Score _____

Review Exercise A for Chapters 11-15
Survival Skills

Prepare a personalized list of the most important considerations as you prepare for an essay examination.

1. _____

2. _____

3. _____

4. _____

5. _____

Review Exercise B for Chapters 11-15
Survival Skills

Prepare a personalized list of the most important considerations as you prepare to submit an essay.

1. _____

2. _____

3. _____

4. _____

5. _____

Chapter 16   Exercise A
Revising Sentence Fragments

The following passage contains fragments. On your own paper, rewrite the passage in complete sentences. Some of the fragments can be combined with independent clauses. For others, you will need to add a subject, a verb, or a new independent clause.

Today, more and more people are becoming interested in discovering their roots. Because of the popularity of a book by Alex Haley, called *Roots*. It tells the story of Haley's search for his ancestors. In Africa and other places. Before he wrote *Roots*, Haley worked on another book. *The Autobiography of Malcolm X*. After *Roots* was published. It became a bestseller. Then they made a movie for television based on it. Now, people of all backgrounds are interested in tracing their ancestry. A good book. A great man.

Chapter 16   Exercise B
Revising Sentence Fragments

The following passage contains fragments. On your own paper, rewrite the passage in complete sentences. Some of the fragments can be combined with independent clauses. For others, you will need to add a subject, a verb, or a new independent clause.

When we moved from an apartment to a house. We discovered that we had more belongings than we thought. So much stuff had to be packed. In the boxes. In suitcases. And even in large garbage bags. We rented a truck. From the local gas station. So we could avoid spending the extra money to hire a mover. We certainly put in a full day's work. That day. Although the process was long and hard. It was worth it.

Chapter 16   Exercise C
Revising Sentence Fragments

Use the conjunctions in parentheses to link the following short sentences or fragments. Rewrite and punctuate as necessary to generate a sentence that is smooth and correct.

Example: You should hurry. We are going to be late. (unless)

Unless you hurry, we are going to be late.

1. The program aired. The executives had debated whether to release it. (after)

_____

_____

2. The dining hall serves three meals a day. Students must eat during the serving hours. (however)

_____

_____

3. The western cowboy. The frontiersman. Blend truth with American mythology. (both, and)

_____

_____

Chapter 16   Exercise D
Revising Sentence Fragments

Use the conjunctions in parentheses to link the following short sentences or fragments. Rewrite and punctuate as necessary to generate a sentence that is smooth and correct.

Example: You should hurry. We are going to be late. (unless)

Unless you hurry, we are going to be late.

1. The officials did not like the thunder that shook the ground and lightning that brightened the sky. The soccer tournament was postponed until Saturday. (because)

_____

_____

2. Erica struck out eleven batters. She hit two doubles and drove in five runs. (not only, but also)

_____

_____

3. The administrators. The faculty. Correctly projected enrollment trends. (neither, nor)

_____

_____

Chapter 17   Exercise A
Revising Comma Splices and Fused Sentences

Correct any run-ons or comma splices by inserting periods, commas, or semicolons as needed.

Example: The porch is sagging the window needs repair.

The porch is sagging; the window needs repair.

The porch is sagging. The window needs repair.

1. Linda is saving her money she wants to travel.

2. Brian could take Staci out for an enjoyable Mexican dinner and a
    movie he has enough money.

3. Clint and Ginger sold their television set now they do not miss it.

4. Don cleaned the apartment he cooked the dinner.

5. In graduate school Louie once studied French and Spanish since
    then he has worked as a translator for the United Nations.

6. When the bridge closed, traffic was slowed for miles even leaving
    early did not help.

7. When you visit our campus for the interview, the most convenient
    parking lot is west of the building ask the attendant for directions
    to my office.

Chapter 17   Exercise B
Revising Comma Splices and Fused Sentences

In the space provided, mark a "C" for a complete sentence or "RO" for a run-on sentence. Draw a line between the independent clauses in run-ons.

1. _____ The president rose to speak, the audience listened.

2. _____ In the waiting room, one woman is writing a letter

   another reading a book about Chartres Cathedral.

3. _____ Brenda is actually the brain of the family's business,

   everyone should realize that by now.

4. _____ The group was small only twelve showed up.

5. _____ Answer, please, as soon as you can.

6. _____ The team has many talented players, Reece is the team's

   dependable shortstop.

7. _____ Ron built the deck, his craftsmanship is truly impressive.

8. _____ I am expecting a call has anyone telephoned?

9. _____ Johnny is respected for his attention to detail, each of his

   customers can be confident about the quality of work he

   provides.

10. _____ Last night I called you, I called several times.

Name _____ Date _____ Score _____

Chapter 17   Exercise C
Revising Comma Splices and Fused Sentences

Correct these run-ons in each of the four ways you have learned.

1. Luke loves golf, he plays a round every sunny day.

a._____

b._____

c._____

d._____

2. Andy collects stamps he probably has that one.

a._____

b._____

c._____

d._____

3. Thomas enjoyed the sailboat he might buy a scooter.

a._____

b._____

c._____

d._____

Chapter 17   Exercise D
Revising Comma Splices and Fused Sentences

On your own paper, revise the following paragraph to change run-ons into complete and correct sentences.

Cats make great pets. You have to be affectionate to them. They are rather independent animals they do not always come when you call them. Many people prefer dogs, you can train them to come, or sit, or fetch a bone. With cats, on the other hand, you have to be willing to let them live their own lives if you attempt to train them you may become discouraged. If you put two cats in the same room, you are in for quite a treat. They chase each other, usually all in fun and when one catches the other the real show begins. Often they will cuddle and clean each other sometimes they will fight. The wise pet owner will know when to break up a fight and when to let it go since it is only play for the cats. They can be great company if you understand them.

    Harcourt, Inc.

Chapter 18   Exercise A
Revising Agreement Errors

Each of these sentences is correct. Read the sentences carefully and explain why each verb form is used in each case.

Example: *Pride and Prejudice* provides valuable insights about life in nineteenth-century England.

(The verb is singular because the subject *Pride and Prejudice* is a title of an individual work, even though it is plural in form.)

1. The children in the audience were mesmerized by the magician's entertaining illusions.

_____

_____

2. Mr. Reidinger's confidence in the benefits of Scouting activities has convinced him to serve as the scoutmaster, even though his son is no longer in the troop.

_____

_____

3. One look at their faces tells you that Angela and Erica enjoy playing softball.

_____

_____

Name _____ Date _____ Score _____

Chapter 18   Exercise B
Revising Agreement Errors

Each of these sentences is correct. Read the sentences carefully and explain why each verb form is used in each case.

Example: *Pride and Prejudice* provides valuable insights about life in nineteenth-century England.

(The verb is singular because the subject *Pride and Prejudice* is a title of an individual work, even though it is plural in form.)

1. Although he fishes often with great success, Mr. Mims seldom comes home with a stringer because he considers "catch and release" to be sportsmanlike.

_____

_____

2. Every coach and player was pleased that the thunderstorm quickly passed through the area.

_____

_____

3. Aerodynamics is extremely important to bicycle design.

_____

_____

Chapter 18   Exercise C
Revising Agreement Errors

Write "C" if the sentence is correct or "X" if it contains an error in agreement. Rewrite incorrect sentences so that subjects and verbs agree.

_____ 1. They make good pizza here.

_____

_____ 2. Everybody know how to work together.

_____

_____ 3. The thunder and lightning was frightening.

_____

_____ 4. Either of the doctors can perform the surgery.

_____

_____ 5. Neither of the animals have been fed.

_____

_____ 6. Each member of the team has a uniform.

_____

_____ 7. You was an excellent worker on that project.

_____

_____ 8. Can you believe the pizzas was late?

_____

Chapter 18   Exercise D
Revising Agreement Errors

On your own paper, rewrite the following passage, changing the subject from a carpenter to carpenters. Keep in mind that verbs and other words that refer to the subject will have to be changed from singular to plural.

A carpenter uses many different tools in his work. When he is faced with a job that is particularly difficult, he has to use his patience as well as his skill. Without patience, a hammer, a saw, or a screwdriver will do a carpenter no good. He has to be able to understand the problem, and find the best way to solve it. Sometimes, the quickest solution is not the best one. His customer, or client, has to be pleased with his work, or he loses his chance to be hired for another job. There is a great pressure on the carpenter to succeed. By no means is his job an easy one.

Chapter 18   Exercise E
Revising Agreement Errors

Double the antecedent for the underlined pronoun in each sentence.

1. Leigh used <u>her</u> pen to write in her notebook.

2. Don wore a jacket over <u>his</u> sweatshirt.

3. Everyone at the party enjoyed <u>her</u> evening.

4. The car has a leak in <u>its</u> transmission.

5. The cow twitched <u>its</u> tail at the fly.

6. Aunt Peggy asked me to catch <u>her</u> dog.

7. My sister earned <u>her</u> doctorate at Florida State.

8. After Grace concluded her recital, the audience applauded <u>her</u>

    performance and hoped for an encore.

9. During winter snowstorms, the sparrows depend on our feeder for

    <u>their</u> food.

10. The rain fell throughout the afternoon; by supper, though, <u>it</u> had

    stopped, so we did not cancel our plans for the evening.

Chapter 18   Exercise F
Revising Agreement Errors

Complete each sentence by underlining the word or phrase that fits logically and clearly.

1. Thirty students have submitted (his / their) lab proposals.

2. Seconds later, Reece grabbed (its / his) backpack and ran.

3. With the hat, Andy wore (her / its) decorative headband.

4. Meg bakes bread that only (her / its) mother can rival.

5. Is Luke's car running (their / its) best this week?

6. My dog sleeps in (its / their) own cozy bed in the garage.

7. Idea became reality when Thomas used (its / his) brain.

8. Of the boys, Nat is most likely to have (his / their) work.

9. Spectacular views are Ronnie's goal on (his / their) hike.

10. Pleasure and confidence are (its / their) own rewards.

Harcourt, Inc.

Chapter 19   Exercise A
Revising Awkward or Confusing Sentences

Review the following sentences for incorrect shifts in tense, person, number, voice, and mood. Underline the mismatched words.

Example: When I <u>tell</u> him that he is cute, he <u>grinned</u>.

1. I close the door because I needed to be left alone.

2. Bill wants to study medicine, but he hated to think of four more years in school.

3. On our trip to Europe last summer, we stay at the best hotels, and we paid the highest prices.

4. Michael washed the dishes and then he begins to bake the cookies.

5. Ed runs well over one hundred miles each week and hoped to qualify for the Olympics.

6. When Reece entered the room, he adjusts the antenna and then changed the channel.

7. Anyone can learn French if they will only try.

8. After one is under water for ten minutes, they will have difficulty breathing.

9. If you adhere strictly to a vegetarian diet, one cannot eat steak, chicken, fish, or pork.

10. In her novel, Jane Austen creates a society that acts according to their characters' social expectations.

Chapter 19   Exercise B
Revising Awkward or Confusing Sentences

On your own paper, rewrite each of the following sentences in two ways to correct the shifts in tense, person, number, voice, and mood.

Example: When I <u>tell</u> him that he is cute, he <u>grinned</u>.
            When I tell him that he is cute, he grins.
            When I told him that he is cute, he grinned.

1. I close the door because I needed to be left alone.

2. Bill wants to study medicine, but he hated to think of four more years in school.

3. On our trip to Europe, we stay at the best hotels, and we paid the highest prices.

4. Michael washed the dishes and then he begins to bake the cookies.

5. Ed runs well over one hundred miles each week and hoped to qualify for the Olympics.

Chapter 19   Exercise C
Revising Awkward or Confusing Sentences

On your own paper, rewrite each of the following sentences in two ways to correct the shifts in tense, person, number, voice, and mood.

Example: When I <u>tell</u> him that he is cute, he <u>grinned</u>.
            When I tell him that he is cute, he grins.
            When I told him that he is cute, he grinned.

1. When Reece entered the room, he adjusts the antenna and then changed the channel.

2. Anyone can learn French if they will only try.

3. After one is under water for ten minutes, they will have difficulty breathing.

4. If you adhere strictly to a vegetarian diet, one cannot eat steak, chicken, fish, or pork.

5. In her novel, Jane Austen creates a society that acts according to their characters' social expectations.

Chapter 19   Exercise D
Revising Awkward or Confusing Sentences

On your own paper, rewrite the following passages to eliminate any incorrect shifts in tense, number, person, voice, or mood.

I work in a bank, and when you have that type of job, you have to be willing to wake up at a very early hour. Each morning, I drive to work, park my car, and walked a block to work. I get a lunch break every day at noon, and they love to eat at the delicatessen around the corner. I worked at the bank for over a year, and decided that I had had enough. After looking around for a new job, I found one where you had to be at work at 6:00 a.m. This job was in a restaurant where you had to stand up all day, and after six months, I decided to go back to the bank. The manager was very nice to me and says, "You can have your old job back if one promises to stay at least two years." I take the job, and I enjoyed an extra hour of sleep every morning.

Chapter 20   Exercise A
Revising Misplaced and Dangling Modifiers

In the space provided, write "C" if the sentence is correct as it stands. Write "DM" if it contains a dangling modifier.

1. _____ Shining brightly in the grass, she stooped to pick up the silver coins that sparkled in the sunlight.

2. _____ While doing my homework, the supper burned.

3. _____ When you are ready, please drive me to school.

4. _____ Running to class, his digital clock pen was lost.

5. _____ The shirt is not only well made, but also attractive.

6. _____ Being antique cut-glass, she handled the bowl carefully as she examined its intricate design.

7. _____ We saw three deer driving through the mountains.

8. _____ Having repaired the outside of the house, the inside needed a great deal of attention as well.

9. _____ To play golf, the eye must be kept on the ball.

10. _____ I sat for an hour, waiting for the lights to go out.

Chapter 20   Exercise B
Revising Misplaced and Dangling Modifiers

On your own paper, rewrite each of the following sentences to correct any faulty modification.

Example: Increasingly   concerned   about   the   environment, conservation has become a hot topic.

Because many people are increasingly concerned about the environment, conservation has become a hot topic. (dependent clause)

1. Although a small part of the world's population, proportionally more of the earth's nonrenewable natural resources are used up by people in developed countries.

2. As fossil fuels, minerals, metals, timber, and water are diminishing, replacement cannot happen because they were built up over billions of years.

3. Doubling every decade, time for change of world consumption of oil would seem short.

4. By flooding certain coastal areas, seawater evaporation extracts a few minerals, such as common salt, magnesium, and bromine.

5. Although polluting the atmosphere, one-half to one-third of the world's additional energy needs in the next twenty years will be satisfied by the use of coal, according to experts.

Chapter 20   Exercise C
Revising Misplaced and Dangling Modifiers

On your own paper, rewrite the following passage, correcting any sentences that contain misplaced modifiers.

These days, many people are trying health foods in all parts of the country. The "back to nature" movement has nearly affected everyone in one way or another. Producers of health foods use no preservatives in their products which they claim are bad for the system. Cereals such as granola a totally natural food are especially popular. People are also eating unstarched rice which is supposed to be good for the digestive system particularly. Ice cream even comes in new, natural flavors such as banana and coconut which is made with fresh bananas. Certainly health food companies are trying hard to attract customers interested in better nutrition.

Chapter 20   Exercise D
Revising Misplaced and Dangling Modifiers

On your own paper, rewrite the following passage, correcting any sentences that contain dangling modifiers.

On arriving in America, the sights and sounds amazed Pierre. Having traveled alone, so many people hurrying around and shouting came as a jolt to him. Coming from a small village in the south of France, so much commotion had never before been witnessed by the young traveler. And being only eight years old and a bit nervous, his luggage seemed to be his only companion. On this trip, his cousins in Philadelphia would be his hosts. After looking for them at the gate, and not being able to find them, an attendant took him to the information booth. Over the loudspeaker, Pierre's cousins were paged. To locate them, an announcement had to be made twice by the attendant. Then, running through the terminal, from the other end of the building, Pierre recognized his relatives. Feeling relieved, Pierre ran to them and escaped the crazy crowds of America.

Review Exercise A for Chapters 16-20
Common Sentence Problems

Label the type of problem found in each of the following entries. For your labels, select from the following list:

comma splice   **fused sentence**
dangling modifier   **agreement error**
sentence fragment

1. On the Philmont trek, each scout packed his own water supply, compass, and rain gear. Also a share of the troop's tents and cooking equipment.

   _____

2. Andy loaded the bottles and cans into his new Porsche, which he planned to leave at the recycling center.

   _____

3. Luke has missed work for seven consecutive days, he's concerned that his job is in jeopardy.

   _____

4. Andy bunted safely three times in yesterday's game he also stole home to score the winning run.

   _____

5. Beth explained, speaking directly to her father, how well she had run her race at the track meet.

_____

6. History can be exciting and engaging too often it is presented in a boring manner.

_____

7. Our family was surprised as we drove through Badlands National Park, the bleak landscape was oppressive.

_____

8. One of my favorite cities in the world is Edinburgh. London, Paris, and Rome, too.

_____

9. Margaret watched the colorful sailboats taking an afternoon jog along the shore.

_____

After thoroughly stirring the batter, making sure that there aren't any lumps in it, two eggs should be cracked into a small bowl. Take care not to break the yolks, and there shouldn't be any pieces of shell in the bowl.

Next, separate the yolks with a small spoon, and store them, since they will not be added to the batter, in an appropriate container. Using a small fork to beat the egg whites will become frothy. Then, combine the egg whites with the batter, mixing them in completely. Preparing the egg whites in this manner, it seems like a waste of time when you could just toss them into the batter. But this way, the waffles turn out with a light texture on the inside and fluffy too.

By this time, the preheating of the waffle iron is probably finished. Some batter should be put in the waffle iron, filling all of the ridges of the iron's bottom side, using a mixing spoon. Now, use a low, medium, or high setting to cook the waffle to your desired preference, golden brown, or for some, burned. These instructions will produce four medium-sized waffles.

Finally, the hardest part of preparing waffles is deciding what topping to use. Whatever topping you decide to use—fruit and cream, butter and syrup, or even ice cream—waffles are always a special, as well as a splendid addition to anyone's breakfast menu treat. Try them sometime.

Review Exercise B for Chapters 16-20
Common Sentence Problems

On your own paper, rewrite the following student draft to eliminate misplaced and dangling modifiers, faulty parallelism, shifts, mixed constructions, and faulty predication. Change and rearrange sentences as necessary.

Making Waffles

After a long night's sleep, how would you like to sit down to a cup of hot coffee and golden brown waffles for breakfast? You would probably like them with warm strawberries and a scoop of fresh, whipped cream, or you prefer the traditional butter and maple syrup. Waffles are, in any case, an excellent breakfast dish, and there are many ways to serve them, for they are easy to prepare. Basically, making waffles involves three steps: preparing the batter, cooking the waffle, and you have to decide how to top it.

First, before mixing the batter is where to preheat the waffle iron. Most irons have to be plugged in, and usually it took from ten to fifteen minutes to heat up. I have found that medium is usually the best setting, but which setting works best for you will have to be decided.

The batter is a relatively simple task. First, combine the following in a large mixing bowl: one cup cake flour, two tablespoons of sugar, two teaspoons of baking powder, and finally add one-fourth teaspoon of salt.

Next, add one cup of milk and one tablespoon of vegetable oil to the dry ingredients. Oil is an important step; otherwise, the waffles will be stuck to the iron. If you don't have any vegetable oil, one tablespoon of melted butter or margarine can be used. Use a medium-sized spoon to stir the batter until it forms without any lumps in it a smooth mixture.

Harcourt, Inc.

After thoroughly stirring the batter, making sure that there aren't any lumps in it, two eggs should be cracked into a small bowl. Take care not to break the yolks, and there shouldn't be any pieces of shell in the bowl.

Next, separate the yolks with a small spoon, and store them, since they will not be added to the batter, in an appropriate container. Using a small fork to beat the egg whites will become frothy. Then, combine the egg whites with the batter, mixing them in completely. Preparing the egg whites in this manner, it seems like a waste of time when you could just toss them into the batter. But this way, the waffles turn out with a light texture on the inside and fluffy too.

By this time, the preheating of the waffle iron is probably finished. Some batter should be put in the waffle iron, filling all of the ridges of the iron's bottom side, using a mixing spoon. Now, use a low, medium, or high setting to cook the waffle to your desired preference, golden brown, or for some, burned. These instructions will produce four medium-sized waffles.

Finally, the hardest part of preparing waffles is deciding what topping to use. Whatever topping you decide to use—fruit and cream, butter and syrup, or even ice cream—waffles are always a special, as well as a splendid addition to anyone's breakfast menu treat. Try them sometime.

Chapter 21   Exercise A
Using Verbs Correctly

Underline the correct verb in each sentence.

1. Although some floats (was / were) ruined by the downpour, the parade began as scheduled.

2. Everybody on the van (want / wants) an order of onion rings and a chocolate milk shake.

3. Although the variety of student backgrounds (make / makes) the class extremely challenging to manage, Mr. Hansard appreciates the stimulating and rewarding class.

4. Each member of the troop realizes that this Eagle Service Project (provide / provides) valuable service to the community.

5. Each member of the committee (has / have) been contacted by the secretary about the next meeting.

6. Many members of the board of directors (think / thinks) that the stock offering will be an immense success.

7. The competition is so keen that neither contestant (wants / want) to give her opponent an advantage.

8. To prepare for the competition, Erica and Beth (ride / rides) their bicycles several miles each day.

9. Every camper (enjoy / enjoys) "water balloon madness," which is the final activity on the first day of camp.

10. Each of the scholars on this school's Science Olympiad team (devote / devotes) a minimum of ten hours of preparation each week by surfing the Internet for helpful sites.

 Harcourt, Inc.

Chapter 21   Exercise B
Using Verbs Correctly

Underline the complete verb of each sentence.

1. Michelle and Mary moved to Hawaii three years ago.

2. Many people knit and sew their own toboggans.

3. There were shadows flickering in the firelight.

4. These candles could light the entire room.

5. Often, though, the candles sputter, flicker, and drip.

6. Jonathan Swift wrote *Gulliver's Travels*.

7. What else did he write?

8. Andrew and Jacob will be responsible for this project.

9. Hot peppers should be used sparingly.

10. What will the future bring?

11. Brian and Beth visited Yosemite National Park.

12. Every Beta Club member hopes to attend the baseball game.

13. Scouts could have served as guides along the path.

14. My computer has crashed only once this week.

15. Most students would prefer to purchase used textbooks.

16. The prowler has been seen in many areas of the neighborhood.

Name _____ Date _____ Score _____

Chapter 21 Exercise C
Using Verbs Correctly

Underline the most logical verb form in each sentence.

1. Marjorie quietly opened the door, pushed her head inside, and (had looked / looked / will look) around the room.

2. If Diane (would have studied / studies / had studied), she would have passed the chemistry semester exam.

3. As you and Michelle must certainly know, for the past two hours I (am / was / have been) busy studying.

4. With several of his neighbors and fraternity brothers, Andrew (celebrate / celebrated / had celebrated) his birthday last night.

5. Before I head for class each morning, I eat breakfast, ride my bicycle, and (do / does / am doing) my exercises.

6. We will try harder, and we (do / did / will do) a much better job next time—if we get the opportunity.

7. The house (is built / was builded / was built) during the terrible heat wave last July and August.

8. Mary tossed the ball, and I (catch / catches / caught) it.

9. Only after he had arrived home from the store did Jacob realize that he (forgot / had forgotten / forgets) to buy bread, milk, eggs, yogurt, and a can of tuna fish.

10. After the performers had taken their final curtain call, the lights in the theater (dim / dimmed / had dimmed).

Chapter 21   Exercise D
Using Verbs Correctly

Complete each sentence by filling in the correct form of the verb in parentheses.

Example: We won the homecoming game last year,
              but we _____*lost*_____ (lose) it this year.

1. Mr. Hansard _____ (escort) a group of

    students to France last year, and he intends _____

    (take) another group to Spain next year. But Brian and Beth

    _____ (wait) one more year for his trip to

    Scotland and England.

2. After I had completed my lab report, I _____ (begin)

    to plan my English essay.

3. Elizabeth would have been prepared for the exam if she

    _____ (listen) to the lectures last week.

4. As I typed my research paper yesterday morning, my roommate's

    cocker spaniel _____ (sit) by my chair.

5. After my grandparents' television set was repaired,

    their stereo _____ (break) down.

Chapter 21   Exercise E
Using Verbs Correctly

Complete the sentences in the following paragraph by inserting the appropriate form (indicative, imperative, or subjunctive) of the verb in parentheses.

Harry Houdini was a famous escape artist. He _____

(perform) escapes from every type of bond imaginable: handcuffs, locks,

straitjackets, ropes, sacks, and sealed chests underwater. In Germany,

workers _____ (challenge) Houdini to escape from a

packing box. If he _____ (can) manage to escape, they

would admit that he _____ (be) the best escape artist in the

world. Before getting into the box, he asked that the observers

_____ (give) it a thorough examination. He then asked that

a worker _____ (nail) him in the box. "_____

(Place) a screen around the box," he ordered after he had been sealed

inside. In a few minutes, Houdini _____ (step) from

behind the screen. When the workers demanded that they

_____ (see) the box, Houdini pulled down the screen. To

their surprise, they saw the box with the lid still nailed tightly in

place.

Name _____ Date _____ Score _____

Chapter 21   Exercise F
Using Verbs Correctly

Determine which sentences in the following paragraph would be more effective in the passive voice. Rewrite those sentences between the lines.

The Regent Diamond is one of the world's most famous and

coveted jewels. A slave discovered the 410-carat diamond in 1701 in an

Indian mine. Over the years, people stole and sold the diamond several

times. In 1717, the Regent of France bought the diamond for an

enormous sum, but during the French Revolution, it disappeared again.

Someone later found it in a ditch in Paris. Eventually, Napoleon had

the diamond set into his ceremonial sword. At last, when the French

monarch fell, the government placed the Regent Diamond in the

Louvre, where it still remains to be enjoyed by all.

Chapter 22   Exercise A
Using Pronouns Correctly

Underline the correct pronoun in each sentence.

1. The cat likes both Megan and (her / she).

2. Two were chosen, Bethany and (he / him), for the team.

3. Having appointed Beth as their representative, every member of the
    club was convinced that (her / she) would represent them well.

4. (He / Him) and Laura played soccer for the same high school.

5. It must be (he / his) car in the driveway.

6. The librarian checked out the videos to (me / I).

7. Royce hates broccoli; it must be (you / yours).

8. We wanted to go shopping with Nancy and (she / her).

9. I gave (he / him) the dog when we moved out of town.

10. Amy counts (they / them) among her best friends.

11. Don asked Amanda and (I / me) for our opinions.

12. The club decided to revise (its / their) schedule.

13. The band's producer and (she / her) have arrived.

14. Fortunately, it was (we / us) who heard the news.

15. The dean approved of (us / our) working together.

Chapter 22   Exercise B
Using Pronouns Correctly

Write a sentence using each of the following word pairs.

Example: computer   its

When the computer crashed for the seventh time this
afternoon, I simply pulled its plug and took a nap.

they   theirs

_____

_____

firefighter   who

_____

_____

technician   she

_____

_____

bicycles   their

_____

_____

Chapter 22   Exercise C
Using Pronouns Correctly

On your own paper, rewrite the following sentences, eliminating any faulty pronoun references.

1. We could not find a parking space, which was why we were late for the surprise party.

2. Travis told Eric that his acceptance speech was one of the best presented following the elections.

3. When Amy put the vase on the mantle, it fell down.

4. Backpacking is Allen's favorite outdoor activity. That is why he spends most weekends in the mountains.

5. When Beth sings that song, it drives her brother crazy.

6. Bev decided not to take the free ride on a hang glider, which allowed Gene to stop worrying.

7. Thomas told Luke that his brother had won first place in the contest for the most original Halloween costume.

8. Andy collects stamps, which provides him with a hobby that he shares with his grandfather.

9. The vocal group of residents convinced the company's board of directors not to build a factory near the town, which gave them a feeling of success.

Chapter 22   Exercise D
Using Pronouns Correctly

Underline the correct word in the parentheses.

1. The members of the singing ensemble agreed to wear (their /

    they're / there) yellow toboggans for tonight's winter concert.

2. (Who's / Whose) team will win the tournament?

3. Who wrote "Beauty is (its / it's) own excuse for being"?

4. (Its / It's) puzzling that Chris hasn't been seen for several days.

5. Most of your classmates confuse you and (your / you're) twin.

6. Vince provided a model for (their / they're / there) design.

7. (Who's / Whose) sitting in that chair by the window?

8. The (governors / governor's) office has been evacuated.

9. (Womens / Women's / Womens') hats were far more popular in

    my grandmother's era.

10. Did you make a good grade on (your / you're) test?

Chapter 23   Exercise A
Using Adjectives and Adverbs Correctly

Underline the adjectives in the following sentences.

1. Clean air is essential if we are to have a safe environment.

2. On the lunar horizon, earth looms blue and cloud-streaked.

3. Whose car did you drive in this relentless downpour?

4. Lost and frightened children always arouse public sympathy.

5. This answer is correct, but that one is not.

6. Although his hair was gray, he was younger than he looked.

7. Did you leave your red umbrella at my house?

8. She was much taller than I.

9. His rumpled clothes and muddy shoes suggested that he had been walking for a long time.

10. The theater was crowded as the first showing ended.

Chapter 23   Exercise B
Using Adjectives and Adverbs Correctly

Complete each sentence by underlining the correct adverb in parentheses.

Example: The artful dodger dodged (<u>more artfully</u> / more artfullier) than the pursuer.

1. The (unique / most unique) shop opened last month.

2. Her embroidery is always (more delicate / more delicatest) than anyone else's.

3. Cindy became (more sick / more sickly) as the cruise continued into its third day.

4. Lynn is the (taller / tallest) of the two roommates.

5. Andy is (heavier / heaviest) than any other member of the state championship wrestling team.

6. Andy is the (heavier / heaviest) member of the state championship wrestling team.

7. David didn't act (grateful / gratefully) for the help.

8. Mocha is the (younger / youngest) of the six pups.

9. Ashley ran a (faster / more fast) mile than anyone else at the region track meet.

10. This unexpected winter storm is now (worse / badder) than it was an hour ago.

Review Exercise A for Chapters 21-23
Sentence Grammar

In the space provided, revise the following student draft to correct errors in pronoun use. Change words and phrases as necessary.

Duck, Duck Goose is a game that children play on a flat surface, usually outside in the grass so you do not get hurt. The first thing you need to do is to put them in a circle so them are sitting down. Choose one to be "it." They will be the first player to choose the "goose." The child whom is "it" will then go around the circle and tap everyone on the head. "It" will say "duck" when they tap them on the head except when they reach one—anyone who they choose. They will tap them on they head and say "goose."

_____

_____

_____

_____

_____

_____

_____

(This exercise continues on the back of this page.)

Harcourt, Inc.

That's when the excitement begins. The "goose" will get up and chase "it" around the outside of the circle until they reach the place where "goose" was sitting and sits down. If "goose" tags "it" before "it" reaches the place where he was sitting, then they have to sit in the middle of the circle that they have made until someone else is tagged by a different "goose." When all of them have had the chance to be the "goose" and "it," then it can end.

_____

_____

_____

_____

_____

_____

_____

_____

_____

Review Exercise B for Chapters 21-23
Sentence Grammar

On your own paper, revise the following student draft to eliminate incorrect, inconsistent, or ineffective verb use. Change words and phrases as necessary.

Dusty

On January 28, 1987, Dusty, my two-year-old Doberman pinscher, was born. Six months following his birth, I begun to train Dusty with Mr. Wagner, a professional dog trainer. After two weeks of obedience training, Dusty learned the "Heel" and "Sit" commands. We worked for four more weeks, spending thirty minutes a day on more basic obedience commands. Dusty, of course, responds very well. Not only he learned all of the obedience commands, but he and I had also built a strong relationship. We were best friends.

During the final week of training, Mr. Wagner says I done more and better with Dusty that he seen anybody else do with their dog since he was in the training business. He said, "I am proud of both your and Dusty's accomplishments."

I felt good about what I had done with Dusty and how all of those obedience commands had been learned by him. Dusty and I continued to work with one another for a year. During that time he starts doing things that I had nothing to do with. For instance, he would attack anyone who threatens to harm me or anybody in my family. If my parents or brothers hit me whenever Dusty was around, Dusty attacks them. Should someone else hit a member of my family, Dusty attack that person. If you drove down our driveway and he didn't recognize your car, he run back and forth in front of it to make you slow down before to reach our yard. People whom he was not familiar with were not allowed to take one step out of their car. Dusty become very well mannered and protective of us.

A year and a half later, a tragedy happens. One summer day, my father is coming down the driveway in a different truck. Dusty hadn't really recognized who was driving the truck or the truck itself, so he darts out in front of it, trying to make it slow down before entering the yard. Unfortunately, the right front wheel hits Dusty in the hind leg and the right back wheel hit him in the head.

Fortunately, Dusty was still alive! No one was allowed to help him but me. Scared to death, I picked him up and he was put in the back of the truck. My second oldest brother rushed Dusty and me to the animal hospital. Dusty's blood is all over my hands and shirt, but I didn't care. All I want was for Dusty has the best medical care possible. Nearly crying, I lifted Dusty back out of the truck and take him inside the animal hospital.

After four days of treatment, the veterinarians allow me to take Dusty home, provided that he would be kept under close supervision. Limping away from the veterinarians, Dusty is eager to get home. It took another two weeks before he has totally healed. After his recovery was made, we continued his training, and he has made even more astonishing accomplishments. I am so proud of Dusty! Now that I am in college I miss him very much, but he will be seen again when I go home.

Chapter 24   Exercise A
Writing Varied Sentences

On your own paper, use coordination, subordination, and embedding to revise this string of choppy simple sentences into a more varied and interesting paragraph.

The Authorized Version of the Bible was first published in 1611. The Authorized Version of the Bible is often referred to as the King James Version. It involved several years of work by numerous scholars. Much of the year prior to its publication was devoted to final preparations. After it had been prepared, the document was sent to press. Many steps were taken during those final months. One step involved calling upon writers of the day. Several of the writers were eminent. They were needed to "refine" this translation. It was the most recent English translation. These writers devoted their efforts to the project. They enhanced the poetic qualities of Proverbs. They enhanced the poetic qualities of the Song of Solomon. And they enhanced the poetic qualities of the Psalms.

Harcourt, Inc.

Chapter 24   Exercise B
Writing Varied Sentences

Complete each of the following steps on your own paper.

A. Combine each of the following sentence groups into one long sentence.
B. Then, compose a relatively short sentence to follow each long one.
C. Finally, combine all the sentences into a paragraph, adding any transitions necessary for coherence. Proofread your paragraph to be sure that the sentences are varied in length.

1. The King James Version of the Bible is the subject of many literary legends. One of the legends is intriguing. It alleges that Shakespeare's hand is present in the King James Version of the Bible. More specifically, though, it alleges that Shakespeare's hand is present in the 46th Psalm.

2. Count to the forty-sixth word from the beginning of the psalm. You will find that it is *shake*. Then identify the forty-sixth word from the end of the psalm. You will find that it is *spear*.

3. The situation becomes even more intriguing. It becomes even more intriguing when we realize that the revision work was underway in 1610. It becomes even more intriguing when we also realize that Shakespeare was forty-six years old in 1610.

Chapter 24   Exercise C
Writing Varied Sentences

On your own paper, revise the compound sentences in this passage so the sentence structure is varied and the writer's meaning and emphasis are clear.

Leonardo da Vinci's *The Last Supper* is one of the most easily recognized works of art. It was produced during Leonardo's residence in Milan. Leonardo was under the patronage of Duke Sforza. Leonardo used oil and tempera for *The Last Supper*. He used a wall in the refectory of Santa Maria della Grazie as his "canvas." Even the most casual art observer has viewed a copy of *The Last Supper*. But few serious students of art realize that it is actually a mural. It measures 14'-5" x 28'. It is surprising that Leonardo completed his work on such a large scale. It is surprising to many who have seen only small replicas. Many of these replicas are the size of a post card.

Chapter 24   Exercise D
Writing Varied Sentences

On your own paper, revise the compound sentences in this passage so the sentence structure is varied and the writer's meaning and emphasis are clear.

Giorgio Vasari records an interesting anecdote. Giorgio Vasari was an Italian art historian. He lived during the sixteenth century. The anecdote concerns Leonardo's use of models. These models were used for *The Last Supper*. Leonardo drew the disciples from life. Leonardo encountered difficulty in locating a suitable Judas Iscariot. While he worked on the painting, Leonardo met with some problems. Leonardo was troubled by the prior of Santa Maria. The prior monitored the work's progress. He monitored from a vantage uncomfortably close for Leonardo. The prior expressed his concerns to Duke Sforza. Leonardo heard that the prior had complained to the duke. Leonardo mentioned that any delay he had experienced was merely the result of his having encountered difficulty in identifying a model. The model was for the betrayer. Leonardo pointed out that he would be delayed no longer. He had located his model. The prior would serve nicely.

Chapter 25   Exercise A
Writing Emphatic Sentences

The following paragraph has both active and passive verbs. On your own paper, rewrite the paragraph using only active verbs.

Conestaga wagons are generally associated with the western frontier, but they were first used in Pennsylvania around 1725. Because heavy supplies were carried well by the wagons, they were used by settlers during the movement west. When the wagons were grouped for traveling, they were called wagons trains. In this way, the plains were crossed safely by many migrants. After the 1850s, the wagons were replaced by the railroads.

Harcourt, Inc.

Name _____ Date _____ Score _____

Chapter 25   Exercise B
Writing Emphatic Sentences

The following paragraph has both active and passive verbs. On your own paper, rewrite the paragraph using only active verbs.

When a European coast was landed on by the Vikings, fear of the Vikings' sudden and fierce raids was learned by the inhabitants. Their high-powered boats were sailed by these Norsemen from Scandinavia to the continent or Britain. The ships were decorated with striped sails and colorful circular shields. Little brightness was brought to the raiders' victims by these ships. A permanent mark was left on the territories that were attacked and occupied with ferocity and persistence by the Vikings. Particularly influenced by their customs and language were Norman France and the region of the British "Danelaw."

Chapter 26   Exercise A
Writing Concise Sentences

On your own paper, rewrite the following paragraph to eliminate wordiness.

When he first began writing, Samuel Clemens incorporated his own experiences that he had had. At one time he worked as a riverboat pilot on the Mississippi River. The pseudonym that he used as a writer, "Mark Twain," came from his experience during those days. This phrase was called out to mark the two-fathom mark on the riverboat line. When the Civil War started, it closed the river. Clemens could no longer pilot riverboats, so he moved west and became a newspaper writer. From his experience as a riverboat pilot, he took along his literary name.

Chapter 26   Exercise B
Writing Concise Sentences

On your own paper, revise the following paragraph to eliminate any unnecessary repetition of words or ideas. Also revise to eliminate deadwood, utility words, or circumlocution.

The seven daughters of Atlas are known as the Pleiades. They were pursued by Orion. Orion was unable to seize any of them. Orion continued to follow them. Orion continued to follow them until Zeus took pity on them. Zeus placed them in the heavens. Seven stars make up the Pleiades constellation. Only six stars are clearly visible. The seventh is invisible except for some people. These people are those who have especially keen vision. In Greek mythology, the seventh star represented Electra. Electra was the mother of Dardanus. Dardanus founded the Trojan race. There is a legend about Electra. The legend held Electra dropped from the sky. Electra did not want to look down from the sky. Electra did not want to see the destruction of Troy. Today, though, all seven stars are visible in the Pleiades. Actually, more than seven stars can be seen. But you must use binoculars to see more than seven stars in this cluster. You can even see several hundred stars. But you must use a telescope. Viewing through a telescope will yield several hundred stars.

Chapter 26   Exercise C
Writing Concise Sentences

On your own paper, revise the rambling sentences in the following paragraph by eliminating excessive coordination and subordination, unnecessary use of the passive voice, and overuse of wordy prepositional phrases and noun constructions. As you revise, make your sentences more concise by deleting nonessential words and superfluous repetition.

Orion lost the trail of the Pleiades. Orion became the companion of Artemis. Artemis was a virgin goddess. Artemis was the goddess of the moon. Artemis was also the twin sister of Apollo. Apollo feared for his sister's chastity. Apollo sent a large scorpion to chase Orion. Orion observed the scorpion enter a body of water. Orion pursued the scorpion. Apollo then persuaded Artemis to shoot the object. The object was bobbing in the waves. Her arrow pierced Orion's head. Artemis was deeply saddened at her loss. Artemis placed Orion's image among the stars. In the stars, Orion's image continues to be stalked by the scorpion. The scorpion is also a constellation. Orion and the scorpion are separated. They are separated by a great distance. The Pleiades, however, are in front of Orion. Orion is much closer to the Pleiades. Orion continues to pursue the Pleiades.

Chapter 26   Exercise D
Writing Concise Sentences

Use sentence combining to rewrite the following paragraph on your own paper so that they are more concise and effective.

Shakespeare had a source for *Macbeth*. The story came from another book. That book was Holinshed's *Chronicles*. There Shakespeare found the tale. He found an account of King Duncan's murder. There he found a suggestion about Lady Macbeth. She was ambitious. There was the story of how Macbeth rose. It also included how he fell.

Chapter 27   Exercise A
Using Parallelism

Underline the word or phrase that maintains the parallel structure in each sentence.

1. At the party, Beth told us of her plans (to leave / and that she was leaving).

2. The more I think about the nuclear issue, the more one question (kept / keeps) entering my mind.

3. Whenever she has a spare moment, Kristi likes to read for entertainment and (enlightenment / to enlighten herself).

4. For months, Kathy's friends have told her that her boyfriend is lazy, poor, and (that he lacked education / uneducated).

5. In Whitney's first letter, she told us that her dormitory room is twelve feet long and (ten feet in length / ten feet wide).

6. Having just finished reading his favorite author's most recent novel, Vernon claims that it is brilliant, informative and (humorous / has a lot of humor).

7. My father likes (the country / to live in the country), to walk in the fields, and to fish in the streams.

8. (You are either late / Either you are late) or I am early.

9. Erica took up painting, writing, and (she taught / teaching) after she left the convent.

10. Dennis was surprised that Trish's favorite hobbies are swimming, playing the guitar, and (riding horseback / to ride horseback).

Chapter 27   Exercise B
Using Parallelism

On your own paper, rewrite each of the following sentences in two ways, using effective and consistent parallelism in your revisions.

Example: Eat, drinking, and be merry.
a. Eat, drink, and be merry.
b. They love eating, drinking, and being merry.

1. Amy Rohling, one of the most talented people we know, is a painter, an actress, and who writes plays.

2. The camera takes clear pictures and that is easy to use.

3. Megan Nelson manages to hold a responsible position, earn an impressive salary, and she is writing a novel.

4. In the recording of popular music, the separate tasks of producing, arranging, and to engineer are often performed by one person who is called the producer.

5. When we are well rehearsed, when our timing is precise, and our singer is in good voice, we sound as good as any other band in the city.

6. On their first date, they were talking, ate, and drinking for hours after most others had left.

7. Laura refuses either to go by bus or by riding the subway.

8. Are marrying, child-rearing, and to shop all there is to life after graduate school?

9. At thirteen months, my grandson Michael exhibits remarkable agility of movement, he comprehends complex ideas, and aggressiveness of character.

Chapter 27 Exercise C
Using Parallelism

Identify the parallel elements in these sentences by underlining parallel words and bracketing parallel phrases and clauses.

Example: Each morning, my roommate amazes me with her energy: she [<u>wakes herself</u> at four o'clock without an alarm], [<u>jogs two miles</u>], [<u>cooks breakfast</u> for both of us], [<u>sends an e-mail</u> to her mother], [<u>calls her boyfriend</u>], and [<u>wears a smile</u> all the while].

1. Brian has developed a challenging training program: before breakfast, he jogs; after lunch, he bikes; and after supper, he swims.

2. Beth and Erica agreed that it was one of the best films they'd seen in several months: its characters were believable, its camera work was intriguing, its soundtrack was spectacular, and its language was inoffensive.

3. Angela worked all of her math problems, studied her Spanish assignment, read two history textbook chapters, and then wrote her composition.

4. Before making the long journey to Panama City Beach for spring break, take these precautions: change the oil, fill the gas tank, check the tires' air pressure, and replace the windshield wipers.

5. For a fishing trip that's certain to be memorable, my grandfather recommends the following preparations: pack your rod, reel, and tackle box; check the boat's motor; purchase gas and oil; and make plenty of peanut butter and jelly sandwiches.

Harcourt, Inc.

Name _____ Date _____ Score _____

On your own paper, revise the following paragraphs, using parallelism and balance whenever possible to highlight corresponding elements and using repetition of key words and phrases to add emphasis. (To achieve repetition, you must change some synonyms.) You may combine sentences, and you may add, delete, or reorder words.

For hundreds and thousands of years, the Nile Valley experienced an annual flood. The yearly floodwaters of the Nile carried soil particles from upstream. The soil particles were deposited throughout the flood plain. The silt deposited by the yearly flood renewed the fertility of the Egyptian fields. This yearly event might be interpreted as a natural disaster. Rather than being a natural disaster, the annual flood permitted the rise of one of the richest of ancient civilizations. It was also one of the most advanced ancient civilizations. The annual flood enabled the people to grow enough food to support a large population. There was enough food for people for other activities. Some of these activities included building, scholarship, and art.

During the past century, the Aswan High Dam was constructed. There have been enormous changes in the Nile Valley. The Aswan High Dam is designed to retain an entire annual flow of the Nile. The Aswan High Dam also provides power to make cheap fertilizers. These fertilizers are needed by the intensively cultivated farms that are no longer covered by silty Nile water, which had previously renewed soil fertility. The Aswan High Dam has ended the annual flooding of the Nile Valley. The Nile used to bring nutritious silt to the region. The nutritious silt was once cherished for its nutrients. Many people now consider the silt a nuisance. The silt is considered a nuisance because it fills up irrigation canals.

Name _____ Date _____ Score _____

Review Exercise A for Chapters 24-27
Sentence Style

1. Revise the following paragraph to eliminate awkward or excessive use of passive constructions.

Jack Dempsey, the heavyweight champion between 1919 and 1926, had an interesting but uneven career. He was considered one of the greatest boxers of all time. Dempsey began fighting as "Kid Blackie," but his career didn't take off until 191 9, when Jack "Doc" Kearns became his manager. Dempsey won the championship when Jess Willard was defeated by him in Toledo, Ohio, in 1919. Dempsey immediately became a popular sports figure; Franklin Delano Roosevelt was one of his biggest fans. Influential friends were made by Jack Dempsey. Boxing lessons were given by him to actor Rudolph Valentino. He made friends with Douglas Fairbanks, Sr., and J. Paul Getty. Hollywood serials were made by Dempsey, but the title his lost by him to Gene Tunney, and Dempsey failed to regain it the following year. Meanwhile, his life was marred by unpleasant developments such as a bitter legal battle with his manager and his 1920 indictment for draft evasion. In subsequent years, after his boxing career declined, a restaurant was opened by Dempsey, and many major sporting events were attended by him. This exposure kept him in the public eye until he lost his restaurant. Jack Dempsey died in 1983.

2. On your own paper, revise the following paragraph to eliminate deadwood, utility words, and circumlocution. When a word is superfluous, delete it or replace it with a more concise expression.

For all intents and purposes, the shopping mall is no longer an important factor in the American cultural scene. In the '80s, shopping malls became gathering places where teenagers met, walkers came to get in a few miles, and shoppers who were looking for a wide selection and weren't concerned about value went to shop. There are several factors that have worked to undermine the mall's popularity. First, due to the fact that today's shoppers are more likely to be interested in value, many of them have headed to the discount stores. Today's shopper is now more likely to shop in discount stores or bulk-buying warehouse stores than in the small, expensive specialty shops in the large shopping malls. Add to this a resurgence of the values of community, and you can see how malls would have to be less attractive than shopping at local stores. Many malls actually have up to 20 percent empty storefronts, and some have had to close down altogether. Others have met the challenge by expanding their roles from shopping centers into community centers. They've added playgrounds for the kids and more amusements and restaurants for the adults. They've also appealed to the growing sense of value shopping by offering gift certificates and discounts to shoppers who spend money in their stores. In the early '90s, it seemed as if the huge shopping malls that had become familiar cultural icons were dying out. Now, it looks as if some of those icons just might make it by meeting the challenges and continue to survive as more than just places to shop.

Review Exercise B for Chapters 24-27
Sentence Style

On your own paper, revise the following student draft to achieve greater sentence variety by varying the length, type, openings, and word order of the sentences.

A Cliffhanger

I slowly opened my eyes. I looked to my right. I could see the huge rocks. They lay awaiting a sacrifice fifty feet below. I looked to my left. I could see the questioning faces peering over the edge of the cliff. I could see snowflakes falling gently around me. Suddenly I came to a realization. Only one thing stood between the boulders and me. It was a gate. I came to another realization at that moment. I knew that skiing was not the sport for me.

It all happened one day in January. I had joined the school ski club. I still don't know why I had joined the ski club, but it seemed like a good opportunity to have fun and meet people. This was our first ski trip.

We rode on a bus to the ski lodge. The ride took an hour. During the ride, I began to worry. I wondered whether I would have been better off missing the trip altogether. I thought about everything that could possibly go wrong; I envisioned myself lying on a hospital bed. I envisioned doctors standing all around. They were trying to revive me. My friends had promised to teach me the basics of the sport. In spite of this, I could foresee a terrifying experience. I was right.

Review Exercise B for Chapters 24-27 (continued)
Sentence Style

We finally reached the lodge. I decided to rationalize. I decided that this is skiing; it's supposed to fun. I was then feeling a bit courageous. I chose to begin on the intermediate slope. I went to the top of the mountain. I looked down the icy terrain. Visions of survival soon faded. A friend offered a few words of encouragement, and I began to conquer the mountain. I went down piece by piece.

I would ski about twenty feet at a time. Then I would stop. That way I would not pick up too much momentum. This process continued with healthy results. Then I reached one particularly demanding part of the slope. It consisted of a sharp drop. It was followed by a ninety-degree turn. I was looking at a deathtrap. It was waiting to engulf me. I said a quick prayer and pushed off. I did not know what lay ahead.

I handled the steep drop with minimal effort. My luck ran out as I attempted to turn. I tried to maneuver around an unsuspecting skier. I lost control. I could not turn. I veered off the ski trail. Of course, I collided with the poor man. I also bent his pole. This seemed trivial to me as I swiftly headed over the side of the cliff. I was in mid-air for a few seconds. I rushed head-on into a gate.

For a few seconds, I lay there in the snow. I was stunned. I did not realize what had happened. Then, I heard my friends calling my name. I heard spectators asking if I were alive. I came back to reality. I had risked my life. I had been participating in something most people call a sport. Fortunately, only my pride was bruised. I will never again slide down mountains on little pieces of wood.

Chapter 28   Exercise A
Choosing Words

On your own paper, rewrite the following paragraphs using standard English forms.

I rides the bus to school. Every morning I walks down to the corner where the bus stop. Usually the bus arrive every twenty minutes. Some days it come late. Yesterday, for example, I waits nearly thirty minutes until it arrived. Once I am on the bus, I usually watches the other riders. They reads they papers or looks out the window. Sometimes I reads until we reaches the campus stop. Then I gets off along with the other students, ready for the first class.

Chapter 28   Exercise B
Choosing Words

On your own paper, rewrite the following paragraphs using standard English forms.

Our neighborhood have many children. Every afternoon, the neighborhood children walks to the playground. If one child have a ball, all the childs tosses it around. If the swings be free, the Colton twins runs over to they. Other childs likes the slide or the sandbox. Although each child have a favorite activity, most of they does nearly everything before it get dark and they has to go home.

Chapter 29   Exercise A
Using a Dictionary

Use a college dictionary to answer the following questions about grammatical form.

1. What are the principal parts of the following verbs:

drink _____

deify _____

carol _____

draw _____

ring _____

2. Some of the nouns in the following list can be used as verbs. Underline those that can be used as verbs.

    canter, minister, council, command, lord, minister, mother

3. What are the plural forms of these nouns?

silo _____

sheep _____

seed _____

scissors _____

genetics _____

alchemy _____

Chapter 29   Exercise B
Using a Dictionary

Use a college dictionary to answer the following questions about grammatical form.

1. What are the comparative and superlative forms of the following adverbs and adjectives?

<u>comparative</u>   <u>superlative</u>

fast _____

airy _____

mere _____

homey _____

unlucky _____

2. Are the following verbs transitive, intransitive, or both?

bias _____

halt _____

dissatisfy _____

turn _____

Chapter 29   Exercise C
Using a Dictionary

Use a college dictionary to find the restrictions on the use of the following words.

1. apse _____

2. bannock _____

3. flunk _____

4. irregardless _____

5. kirk _____

6. lorry _____

7. sine _____

8. whilst _____

Chapter 29   Exercise D
Using a Dictionary

Consult a dictionary to help you divide each of these words into syllables. Then indicate with a hyphen where you would divide each word at the end of a line.

Example:

underground   un • der • ground   under-ground

1. amazing _____

2. bookkeeper _____

3. calliope _____

4. longitude _____

5. markedly _____

6. martyr _____

7. side-splitting _____

8. thorough _____

9. transcendentalism _____

10. unlikely _____

Chapter 29   Exercise E
Using a Dictionary

To test the research capability of your dictionary, use it to answer the
following questions.

1.   In what year did Anwar el-Sadat win the Nobel Peace Prize?

_____

2.   After whom was the Ferris wheel named?

_____

3.   What is the atomic weight of sulfur? _____

4.   What is the full name of the French playwright known as Molière?

_____

5.   Define *surrealism*?

_____

_____

Chapter 29   Exercise F
Using a Dictionary

Using your college dictionary, look up the etymologies of the following words. How does the history of each word help you remember its definition?

1. mountebank

2. pyrrhic

3. pittance

4. protean

5. fathom

6. gossamer

7. rigmarole

8. maudlin

Chapter 30   Exercise A
A Glossary of Usage

Underline the correct word in the parentheses.

1. In ancient times, a comet signaled (eminent / imminent) danger.

2. The red convertible must have been going eighty miles per hour when it (passed / past) us on the freeway.

3. My dog (sits / sets) under our oak tree hoping to catch a squirrel.

4. The club's Code of Conduct embodies specific (principals / principles) that each member is expected to uphold.

5. After asking for clarification on the point, the judge directed the attorney to (precede / proceed).

6. Kenjy's grandparents (emigrated / immigrated) from Japan.

7. Laura's recovery seems much (farther / further) along than the doctors had anticipated.

8. While some people are convinced that Kentucky's (capital / capitol) is Louisville and others thinks it's Lexington, you'll have to visit Frankfort to find the governor in the (capital / capitol) building.

9. Although the retired general has (less / fewer) power than he once possessed, he's fortunate that he also has (less / fewer) worries and obligations.

10. Did you make a good grade on (your / you're) test?

Chapter 30   Exercise B
A Glossary of Usage

Underline the correct word in the parentheses.

1. Although your essay is three days late, your instructor will probably (accept / except) it, but she'll likely penalize it.

2. If you want the penalty to have less (affect / effect), you should submit the essay as soon as possible.

3. (Who's / Whose) team will win the tournament?

4. Dee's poem makes an (allusion / illusion) to the seven deadly sins.

5. (Its / It's) puzzling that Mitzi hasn't been seen for several days.

6. Most of your classmates confuse you and (your / you're) twin.

7. Lochlin provided a model for (their / they're / there) design.

8. The three parties agreed (among / between) themselves to settle the case.

9. Kelsey's gymnastics coach (complemented / complimented) her for showing excellent improvement.

10. Hoyt has requested to remain (conscience / conscious) throughout the entire procedure.

Review Exercise A for Chapters 28-30
Using Words Effectively

1. You've just returned from your month-long trip to the location of
   your choice. As a graduation gift, your wealthy aunt let you select
   your destination—anywhere in the world—and paid all of your
   expenses. In the space below, use diction appropriate for your
   friends to write a one-paragraph description of your vacation.

   _____

   _____

   _____

   _____

   _____

   _____

   _____

   _____

   _____

   _____

   _____

   _____

   _____

   _____

2. In the space below, write another one-paragraph description of your vacation; in this account, however, use diction appropriate for your wealthy aunt, who wants to hear the details. Remember that she's former president of the local chapter of the Daughters of the American Revolution. By the way, when you're speaking with your aunt, two of her closest friends will be present in your aunt's parlor.

_____

_____

_____

_____

_____

_____

_____

_____

_____

_____

_____

_____

_____

_____

Review Exercise B for Chapters 28-30
Using Words Effectively

On your own paper, revise the following student draft for appropriateness, accuracy, and freshness. Where appropriate, include figurative language. Change words and rewrite sentences as necessary. [Note that this exercise continues on the back of this page.]

Pilot Mountain

My favorite place is a unique mountain surrounded by trees. Its beauty is better than all the modernization of man below it. It has a unique rock formation. Nowhere on this earth can you find another such creation that could even compare.

_____

_____

_____

_____

_____

_____

_____

_____

_____

Review Exercise B for Chapters 28-30 (continued)
Using Words Effectively

The Little Pinnacle is where you want to look at the knob.
Through all the mountain's original symmetry, the Little Pinnacle still
remains the most breath-taking point. To reach this point, one must
climb a long path full of lots of obstacles. After the hike one can rest on
a rock and marvel at the wonders of nature.

_____

_____

_____

_____

_____

The most famous point on the mountain is the Knob. Looking
from the Little Pinnacle, one can see lots of tall, straight trees growing
on top of the Knob. The walls of the Knob are stone. No plants grow
there. It all looks pretty funny. You can see the Knob from lots of other
places in the area, but this view is still the best.

_____

_____

_____

_____

_____

_____

Chapter 31   Exercise A
End Punctuation

Correct these sentences by adding missing periods and by deleting
unnecessary periods. If a sentence needs no changes, write *correct*.

Example: Dr Dan Drinnon examined his patient in the I.C.U. prior
to recommending the emergency surgery

Dr. Dan Drinnon examined his patient in the ICU prior to
recommending the emergency surgery.

1.   Students are sometimes confused by the graduation requirements
for the AA, the AS, and the AAS

2.   Having gone through rigorous training, they were prepared now for
their work in the Peace Corps

3.   Have most of the faculty earned the M.A.?

4.   After she graduated from F.S.U. with a J.D, she interviewed with
N.A.S.A. in Florida with the J.P.L. in California.

5.   The President's press conference at D.O.E. was scheduled for 10
am, but it was postponed until 2 pm

Chapter 31   Exercise B
End Punctuation

Correct the use of question marks in the following sentences. If a sentence needs no changes, write *correct*.

Example: Kate asked whether the game had been postponed because of the thunderstorm?

Kate asked whether the game had been postponed because of the thunderstorm.

1. Lochlin wondered whether he should take a nine o'clock class?

2. The instructor asked, "Was the Spanish-American War a victory for America?"?

3. Are they really going to jump from that bridge???

4. Hoyt took a modest (?) portion of dessert—half a pie.

5. "Is *data* the plural of *datum*?," he inquired.

Chapter 31   Exercise C
End Punctuation

Correct the use of exclamation points in these sentences.

Example: Caught up in the excitement of the game, the announcer
            shouted, "What a spectacular shot."

            Caught up in the excitement of the game, the announcer
            shouted, "What a spectacular shot!"

1. Are you kidding?! I never said that.

2. When the cell divided, each of the daughter cells had an extra
    chromosome!

3. This is fantastic. I can't believe you bought this for me.

4. Wow!! Just what I always wanted!! A red Mustang!!

5. "Eureka!," cried Archimedes as he sprang from his bathtub.

Chapter 31   Exercise D
End Punctuation

Add appropriate punctuation to this passage. Write your changes between the lines.

Dr Bertram Davis and his group of divers paused at the shore, staring respectfully at the enormous lake Who could imagine what terrors lay beneath its surface Which of them might not emerge alive from this adventure Would it be Col Jim Riser, chief scientist for the Royal Navy; Capt John Fenstermaker, the director of security at the naval base; or Dr Anne Rowe, author of numerous articles and books Or would they all survive the task ahead Dr Davis decided some encouraging remarks were in order

"Attention divers," he said in a loud, forceful voice "May I please have your attention The project that we are about to undertake—"

"Oh, no" screamed Ms Fox suddenly "Look out It's the Loch Ness Monster"

"Quick" shouted Dr Davis "Move away from the shore" But his warning came too late

Chapter 32   Exercise A
The Comma

In the space provided, write "C" if the sentence is punctuated correctly or "X" if it contains an error in comma usage.

1. _____ They went to London, where they saw the queen.

2. _____ I called my sister last night and told her that I might be late for Thanksgiving dinner but I would be there before sunset.

3. _____ Before Richard knew it, the game was over.

4. _____ Until Matt decides to study, he will continue to fail.

5. _____ After he decides to study his grades will begin to improve.

6. _____ Although the salary is low, Joel likes to work.

7. _____ Although Cliff was much in debt, he entered the bank with the air of a conqueror.

8. _____ Kelsey tore up her first three drafts, because she wanted the letter to be perfect.

9. _____ The parlor, large and luxurious, was beautifully furnished.

10. _____ An old man, who had a broken leg, opened the gates.

Chapter 32   Exercise B
The Comma

Insert any missing commas.

Example: My opinion inasmuch as you asked is that the expedition
             is likely to succeed.

             My opinion, inasmuch as you asked, is that the expedition
             is likely to succeed.

1. Beth's report made it clear that her four favorite artists are Monet
    Renoir Degas and Manet.

2. Let Brian and Angela our most skillful speakers present our
    proposal to the board of directors.

3. Long regarded as a leading newspaper the *Washington Post* boasts
    an outstanding staff of reporters.

4. Slowly slyly and cautiously Eric slid the wallet across the kitchen
    table.

5. During Louie's sophomore year in high school he read *As You
    Like It Julius Caesar Romeo and Juliet* and *Hamlet*.

6. I believe that is the book.

7. I believe that but it is an unusual excuse.

8. I believe that a dozen eggs will make quite a mess.

9. The elephant that stands on the drum is Maggie.

10. The elephant which is a hard worker and a talented performer is
    found in most zoos and circuses.

Chapter 32   Exercise C
The Comma

The following sentences contain errors in the use of commas. Insert a comma as necessary. Circle any comma that should be deleted.

1. Once upon a time there was a dog that could fly.

2. We met as usual at the corner of Hollywood, and Vine.

3. I waited, for nearly a month for your letter.

4. It is my choice however to travel alone.

5. For once try studying.

6. You are mine and I am yours.

7. Write to me at 65 Market Street Portland Maine.

8. You are all prepared I'm sure for the test.

9. Ice cream if it is made at home is very good.

10. As long as I live I will love to dance.

Chapter 32   Exercise D
The Comma

The following sentences contain errors in the use of commas. Insert a comma as necessary. Circle any comma that should be deleted.

1. Waving her wand the good fairy performed some magic.

2. Never never will you get away with that.

3. I had a bacon lettuce and tomato sandwich for lunch.

4. Who in your opinion is the world's greatest athlete?

5. Her latest poem, is superb.

6. As of next week the prisoner will be a free man.

7. His answer which was wrong made the class laugh.

8. That dog barking at the tree, is mine.

9. We were wed on March 18 1939.

10. When our guests arrived we greeted them at the door.

Chapter 33   Exercise A
The Semicolon

Replace commas with semicolons where necessary to separate internally punctuated items in a series.

1. Research on animals' ability to think has been conducted on dolphins, who often respond to communicative gestures, sea lions, who seem to show some understanding of logical relationships between symbols, and parrots, who can be taught vocabulary.

2. Business letters should be written with a personal, courteous tone, best achieved through the use of the word *you*, a positive tone, easily created by rephrasing negative statements, and a natural tone, the result of using language that is intended to express, not impress.

3. Engaging in aerobic exercise results in benefits to the cardiovascular system, an increase in stamina, an important physical asset in today's fast-paced lifestyle, and an overall sense of well-being.

Name _____ Date _____ Score _____

Combine each of the following sentence groups into one sentence that contains only two independent clauses. Use a semicolon to separate the two clauses. You may need to add, delete, relocate, or change some words; keep experimenting until you find the arrangement that best conveys the meaning of the group of sentences. Your answers may vary from the model answer.

Example: In the springtime, birds nest in the fir tree in my back yard. I see fluttering chickadees. I see bold cardinals.

In the springtime, birds nest in the fir tree in my backyard; I see fluttering chickadees and bold cardinals.

1. Television soap operas provide a diversion to real life. Soap opera characters are often wealthy. The never seem to work.

_____

_____

2. Ads on afternoon soap operas are directed primarily toward women. The viewer rarely sees ads for men on afternoon soap operas. These ads include soap, toothpaste, skin creams, and nail products.

_____

_____

Chapter 33   Exercise C
The Semicolon

Combine each of the following sentence groups into one sentence that contains only two independent clauses. Use a semicolon to separate the two clauses. You may need to add, delete, relocate, or change some words; keep experimenting until you find the arrangement that best conveys the meaning of the group of sentences. Your answers may vary from the model answer.

Example: In the springtime, birds nest in the dogwood tree in my back yard. I see fluttering chickadees. I see bold cardinals.

In the springtime, birds nest in the dogwood tree in my backyard; I see fluttering chickadees and bold cardinals.

1.   Hale-Bopp was an extraordinary comet. It was seen by millions of ordinary people. It was visible at sunrise and sunset in the spring of 1997 throughout the United States.

_____

_____

2.   The United States Capitol is at one end of the Mall. The Washington Monument is at the other end. Both visitors and residents use the space between the two for volleyball, sunbathing, and strolling.

_____

_____

Chapter 33   Exercise D
The Semicolon

Combine each of the following sentence groups into one sentence that includes a series of items separated by semicolons. You may need to add, delete, relocate, or change words. Try several versions of each sentence until you find the most effective arrangement.

Example: The flag of each Scandinavian country depicts a cross on a solid background. Denmark's flag is red with a white cross. Norway's flag is also red, but its cross is blue, outlined in white. Sweden's flag is blue with a yellow cross.

The flag of each Scandinavian country depicts a cross on a solid background: Denmark's flag is red with a white cross; Norway's flag is also red, but its cross is blue, outlined in white; and Sweden's flag is blue with a yellow cross.

1. A good dictionary offers definitions of words, including some obsolete and nonstandard words. It provides information about synonyms, usage, and word origins. It also offers information on pronunciation and syllabication.

_____

_____

2. Collecting baseball cards is a worthwhile hobby. It helps children learn how to bargain and trade. It also encourages them to assimilate, evaluate, and compare data about major league ball players. Perhaps most importantly, it encourages them to find role models in the athletes whose cards they collect.

_____

_____

Chapter 34   Exercise A
The Apostrophe

Insert missing apostrophes in the following sentences.

Example: Its a shame that your ring is lost.

It's a shame that your ring is lost.

1. Im not going out in that blizzard.

2. Have you corrected Karens homework yet?

3. Genes store specializes in mens clothing.

4. Allens store carries only boys clothes.

5. My brother-in-laws job is with the county clerks office.

6. Frances and Englands agreement was offset by Japans secret pact
    with Germany.

7. Watch your Ps and Qs at Grandmas house.

8. Johns condition results entirely from neglect.

9. Bev is going on a weeks vacation.

10. Well go if youll stay with the baby.

Harcourt, Inc.

Chapter 34   Exercise B
The Apostrophe

Insert missing apostrophes in the following sentences.

Example: Wheres the monkeys toy?

Where's the monkey's toy?

1. Im just a person who cant say no.

2. The childs role is to play the Spirit of 76.

3. His bachelors degree is from his countrys only university.

4. Tally the Ys here and the Ns there.

5. Oohs and ahs rose from the astonished audience.

6. For an hours labor, Lochlin earned a days pay.

7. I wanted to hear yess, but all I heard were maybes.

8. Does Sarah know her ABCs already?

9. The Cowarts home is just around the corner.

10. Amys apartment is upstairs; Jessicas is downstairs.

11. What will the class of 73 plan for the reunion?

12. The five partners signatures were necessary.

13. Shes home, but hes working at a childrens camp.

14. "Well, well have to honor his last will if were to divide the estate

now," said the attorney.

Chapter 35   Exercise A
Quotation Marks

Insert missing quotation marks or other related punctuation in the sentences that follow.

1. Where do you think you're going she demanded.

2. Yogi Berra said It ain't over till its over.

3. "A Philmont Experience" is the cover story in the June edition of *Scouter Magazine*.

4. Can you Yanks tell me said the British officer where to find your commanding officer

5. Hemingways *Men without Women* included the story In Another Country.

6. Dover Beach is one of Matthew Arnold's best-known poems.

7. Who said Yes

8. Open your blue books said the professor and begin your exam.

9. The rain has ruined our ski trip complained Megan.

10. We will meet again in two weeks said the professor as the class began to leave.

Chapter 35   Exercise B
Quotation Marks

Add single and double quotation marks to these sentences where necessary to set off direct quotations from identifying tags.

Example: Gertrude Stein said, You are all the lost generation.

Gertrude Stein said, "You are all the lost generation."

1. Freedom of speech does not guarantee anyone the right to yell Fire!

    in a crowded theater, she explained.

2. To many freshmen, social security means a date for Saturday night.

3. Wordsworth's phrase splendour in the grass was used as the title

    of a movie about young lovers.

4. *Beside* means next to, but *besides* means except.

5. If everyone will sit down, the teacher announced, the exam will

    begin.

Chapter 36   Exercise A
Other Punctuation Marks

Circle the correct punctuation mark given in the parentheses.

1. I have never been to England (; / :) it is supposed to be lovely.

2. It is lovely in three seasons (; / :) spring, summer, and fall.

3. Winter is not so lovely (; / :) it is cold and windy then.

4. It may be cold, and it may snow (; / :) nevertheless, I can have fun in the winter.

5. In winter I enjoy the following (; / :) skiing, skating, and tobogganing.

6. I also like summer sports (; / :) swimming, riding, hiking.

7. Winter in England is the time for sleigh rides (; / :) summer is the time for hayrides.

8. I used to enjoy staying home (; / :) now I would like to travel.

9. I would enjoy visiting many lands (; / :) France, England, Italy, Norway, Switzerland.

10. There are two pleasures to traveling (; / :) seeing new faces, and visiting new places.

Harcourt, Inc.

Chapter 36   Exercise B
Other Punctuation Marks

Correct any errors in the use of semicolons or colons. Insert your corrections within the paragraph.

The team was in trouble, it had dropped from first place to last in three weeks. The manager called a meeting of the players at which the following issues were discussed; the importance of developing a winning attitude, whereby the players would place the goals of the team over their individual achievements, the imposition of a strict curfew so that the players would be well rested for the games, the problem of teammates competing among themselves for higher salaries and greater coverage in the newspapers, and last but not least, the general lack of hustle and determination on the part of the team's stars.

Chapter 36   Exercise C
Other Punctuation Marks

Add dashes where needed in the following sentences.

Example: World War I called "the war to end all wars" was,
unfortunately, no such thing.

World War I—called "the war to end all wars"—was,
unfortunately, no such thing.

1. Tulips, daffodils, hyacinths, lilies all of these beautiful flowers

grow from bulbs.

2. St. Kitts and Nevis two tiny island nations are now independent

after 360 years of British rule.

3. "But it's not" She paused abruptly and reconsidered her words.

4. He considered several different majors history, English, political

science, and business before deciding on journalism.

5. The two words added to the Pledge of Allegiance in the 1950s

"under God" remain part of the Pledge today.

Harcourt, Inc.

Chapter 36   Exercise D
Other Punctuation Marks

Add parentheses where needed in the following sentences.

Example: The greatest battle of the War of 1812 the Battle of New
Orleans was fought after the war was declared over.

The greatest battle of the War of 1812 (the Battle of New
Orleans) was fought after the war was declared over.

1. George Orwell's *1984* 1949 focuses on the dangers of a totalitarian
society.

2. The final score 56-0 was a devastating blow for the Wildcats.

3. Hoyt told us that Belize formerly British Honduras offers
spectacular off-shore diving opportunities.

4. The first phonics book *Phonics Is Fun* has a bright blue cover.

5. Some high school students participate in so many extracurricular
activities band, sports, drama club, and school newspaper, for
instance that they have little time to study.

Chapter 36   Exercise E
Other Punctuation Marks

Add appropriate punctuation—colons, dashed, parentheses, brackets, or slashes—to the following sentences. Be prepared to explain why you chose the punctuation marks. Write your changes in or between the lines.

Example: There was one thing she was sure of if she did well at the interview, the job would be hers.

There was one thing she was sure of: If she did well at the interview, the job would be hers.

1. Mark Twain Samuel L. Clemens made the following statement " I

can live for two months on a good compliment."

2. Saudi Arabia, Oman, Yemen, Qatar, and the United Arab Emirates

all these are located on the Arabian Peninsula.

3. John Adams 1735-1826 was the second president of the United

States; John Quincy Adams 1767-1848 was the sixth.

4. The sign said "No tresspassing *sic*."

Chapter 36   Exercise F
Other Punctuation Marks

Add appropriate punctuation—colons, dashed, parentheses, brackets, or slashes—to the following sentences. Be prepared to explain why you chose the punctuation marks. Write your changes in or between the lines.

Example: There was one thing she was sure of if she did well at the interview, the job would be hers.

There was one thing she was sure of: If she did well at the interview, the job would be hers.

1.   *Checkmate* a term derived from the Persian phrase meaning "the

king" is dead announces victory in chess.

2.   The following people were present at the meeting the president of

the board of trustees, three trustees, and twenty reporters.

3.   Before the introduction of the potato in Europe, the parsnip was a

major source of carbohydrates in fact, it was a dietary staple.

4.   Liza Minnelli, the actress singer who starred in several films, is the

daughter of Judy Garland.

Name _____ Date _____ Score _____

Review Exercise A for Chapters 31-36
Understanding Punctuation

On your own paper, rewrite the following passage, inserting or revising periods, commas, exclamation points, question marks, and quotation marks.

Three men were stationed in the farthest reaches of Alaska, and their supply of orange juice was running low. Two of the men felt that they could take advantage of the third, so they told him to go out into the blizzard and buy some more orange juice in the nearest town. The third man said I will go only if you promise to save the last drop of this remaining orange juice for me. Don't worry the others said we promise. I will definitely not go if you drink that last drop the third man said. We promise, we promise, the others assured him. With that, the third man left. A day went by Two days went by A week and then two weeks went by. The two men figured that the third must have died in the blizzard so they decided "to drink the last bit of orange juice." They took the bottle from the refrigerator, said Cheers, and were about to indulge when the third man flung the door open. I told you he announced I wasn't going to go if you drank that last drop!

Name _____ Date _____ Score _____

Review Exercise B for Chapters 31-36
Understanding Punctuation

On your own paper, rewrite the following paragraphs so that they are properly punctuated.

Small towns and cities especially older ones face difficult financial problems Their revenues are limited but they're expected to maintain service levels despite added costs Sometimes the size of a towns annual budget is restricted by the state in other cases the local officials determine its size Ultimately such budgets are limited by the ability and willingness of citizens to pay the property taxes that generally fund such municipalities.

When a municipal budget is strained officials have two choices increase revenues or cut expenditures In the past extra funds came from the state and federal governments but now many towns must do without such aid Instead increased revenues can come only from new homes whose owners pay property taxes new or revitalized businesses whose tax bills rise with their revenues or new industry whose taxes are a function of space occupied and revenues.

In an older town however with little vacant land not much new growth can be encouraged In addition revitalizing an old run down business district requires time capital and community support Thus if revenues cant or dont grow towns have no choice but to cut their expenses.

How can a town or small city spend less One city manager summed up the problem when he said Were like a business during tough times We have to be more efficient more careful with our pennies and more concerned about our customers the demanding overburdened taxpayers who depend on our services And how does a town accomplish this Few communities have long-term answers for many fixed costs pensions utilities insurance and the like are beyond their control.

Chapter 37   Exercise A
Spelling

Write "C" if the word is correctly spelled. If it is misspelled, write it correctly in the space provided.

1. Wendsday   _____

2. arrangment   _____

3. couragously   _____

4. simular   _____

5. applyed   _____

6. potatos   _____

7. admitance   _____

8. hinderence   _____

9. athelete   _____

10. kindergarden _____

11. exaduration   _____

12. suprize   _____

13. enterance   _____

14. eventhough   _____

Chapter 37   Exercise B
Spelling

Underline the correctly spelled word in the parentheses.

1. Jonna will not (except / accept) his present.

2. Vince's hard work (affected / effected) his grades.

3. Raleigh is the (capital / capitol) city of North Carolina.

4. Don't just (lay / lie) there; hop up and answer the phone.

5. To Jim's surprise, no one was (their / there).

6. We allow no (acception / exception) to this rule.

7. Did you (lose / loose) your wallet?

8. Don't forget to renew your driver's (license / lisense).

9. (Driveing / Driving) without one is a crime.

10. If you have renewed it (already / allready), don't worry.

11. Don't drive without it in your (posession / possession).

12. Some (friendly / freindly) officer might ask to see it.

Chapter 38   Exercise A
Capitalization

Correct any capitalization errors—lower-case letters that should be capitals or capitals that should be lower case.

        aunt   February
Example: My Aunt always gets depressed in february.

1. The Professor who taught english 202 changed my attitude about reading the Poetry of alexander pope and robert frost.

2. Swedish tennis pro Bjorn Borg, who won the wimbledon title that year, lost the U.S. Open Championship at flushing meadow stadium.

3. When Whitney was at harvard, I used to take the amtrak train to Boston every friday to visit her.

4. The statue of liberty was closed when i was in new york, but i still took the Ferry boat to ellis island.

5. The Articles of Confederation preceded the constitution of the United States and the bill of rights.

Chapter 38   Exercise B
Capitalization

Correct any capitalization errors—lower-case letters that should be capitals or capitals that should be lower case.

Lucky Chance Grill
Example: Working at the lucky chance grill has educated me

human nature
about Human Nature.

1. When Fall arrives, the children—angela, erica, beth, and

   brian—begin to plan for halloween.

2. We drove up maple street until we came to the Highway and

   turned North toward cumberland state park.

3. Professor andrew luke thomas explained that Siddhartha, called the

   buddha, founded buddhism in india.

4. Many americans faced hard times when the roaring twenties gave

   way to the great depression.

5. Our assignment is to read george eliot's *middlemarch*.

6. The mayflower compact established a government for plymouth

   colony.

7. On a clear Summer evening, we can see the big dipper in the sky.

Chapter 39   Exercise A
Italics

Underline any words that should be italicized.

Example: Year after year, new parents turn to Dr. Spock's <u>Baby and Child Care</u>.

1. Because it is extremely challenging, William Faulkner's <u>The Sound and the Fury</u> is one of those novels that I have enjoyed reading multiple times.

2. Lincoln first gave his Gettysburg Address at the dedication of a cemetery.

3. For many people, the word <u>cavalry</u> is a tongue twister.

4. When the Supreme Court decided <u>Marbury v. Madison</u>, it established the right of judicial review.

5. The hero of <u>Beowulf</u>, a long epic poem in Old English, dies fighting a dragon.

6. <u>The Thinker</u> is Rodan's best-known sculpture.

7. When <u>Sesame Street</u> was first broadcast, it challenged conventional ideas about children's television.

8. The drama group presented Shakespeare's <u>Romeo and Juliet</u> in modern dress.

9. She can call him or vice versa.

10. <u>Cyperus papyrus</u> was used in ancient Egypt for fuel, food, fabric, and paper.

Chapter 39   Exercise B
Italics

Underline any words that should be italicized.

Example: Year after year, new parents turn to Dr. Spock's <u>Baby and Child Care</u>.

1.   I always have trouble pronouncing the word schism.
2.   He wrote there, but he meant their.
3.   She call is strombis pugilis; I call it a pretty shell.
4.   I read the Los Angeles Times every day, but I also like the weekly coverage in Newsweek.
5.   Stadman's article on Dutch Protestantism appeared in the Sixteenth Century Journal.
6.   A similar argument, "Patterns of Worship in Flanders," appeared in Renaissance Studies.
7.   An Atlantic crossing on a Concorde is nothing like one was on the Mayflower.
8.   The word canteen, derived from the Italian cantina, has been used in English since the eighteenth century.
9.   The giant panda, Ailuropoda melanoleuca, is related not to the bear but to the raccoon.
10. The choir presents Handel's Messiah each year.

Chapter 40   Exercise A
Hyphens

Form compound adjectives from the following word groups, inserting hyphens where necessary.

Example: a contract for three years

                 a three-year contract

1. a relative who has long been lost

2. someone who is addicted to video games

3. a salesperson who goes from door to door

4. a display calculated to catch the eye

5. friends who are dearly beloved

6. a household that is centered on the child

7. a line of reasoning that is hard to follow

8. the border between Tennessee and Kentucky

9. a candidate who is forty-four years old

10. a computer that is friendly to its users

    Harcourt, Inc.

Name _____ Date _____ Score _____

Add hyphens to the compounds in these sentences wherever they are necessary. Consult a dictionary if necessary.

Example: Alaska was the forty ninth state to join the United States.

Alaska was the forty-ninth state to join the United States.

1. My pre certification class has fifty three students on the roster, but only thirty seven have shown up.

2. By emphasizing her position as a middle of the road independent, the little known candidate hopes to win the runoff.

3. One of the restaurant's blue plate specials is chicken fried steak.

4. Both Texas and Virginia are right to work states.

5. Don stood on tiptoe to see the near perfect statue, which was well hidden by the security fence.

6. The new store in the mall has a self service makeup counter and stocks many up to the minute gadgets.

7. The so called Saturday night special is opposed by pro gun control groups.

8. For his pre-game meal, he ordered two all beef patties with special sauce, lettuce, cheese, pickles, and onions on a sesame seed bun for his pre game meal.

9. Although last night's speaker presented some thought provoking insights, he hardly presented any earth shattering conclusions.

10. The Braves Mets game was rained out, so the long suffering fans left for home.

Chapter 41   Exercise A
Abbreviations

In the space provided below each sentence, correct any abbreviations that should be spelled out or any words that would be abbreviated in an essay.

1. Of the three bros., Wm. Collins, Junior, is obviously tallest, standing 6 ft. 11 ins. in his stocking feet.

_____

2. In his address to the Corps of Cadets last Thurs., Gen. Ross announced a 12% increase in dessert expenditures.

_____

3. Although Meg mailed the two letters on the same day at an Atlanta post office, she was surprised that one letter arrived in CA two days before the other arrived in FL.

_____

4. The phone calls for Ms. Davis came from Prof. Bollman in NY, from Sen. Nelson in Washington, District of Columbia, and from Gov. Andrews in AZ.

_____

_____

5. After taking my bus. admin. final exam, I returned to my dorm room & found a note that read, "See you this aft. when yr. tests are thru."

_____

_____

Chapter 41   Exercise B
Abbreviations

In the space provided below each sentence, correct any abbreviations that should be spelled out or any words that would be abbreviated in an essay.

1. Saint Valentine, martyred c. 270, is remembered thru-out the world each year on Feb. 14.

_____

2. When it is 1 p.m. EST, it is only 11 a.m. MST.

_____

3. With her M.A., Beth intends to teach at the local jr. coll. for a few years, but she hopes to earn her doctorate so she can move to a major univ. near her hometown in TN.

_____

_____

4. That section of Intro. to Shakespeare meets Mon., Wed., & Fri. at 11 a.m. in the Gabehart Memorial Bldg.

_____

_____

5. Today I have anthro. at 8 a.m., but my 10 a.m. lit. course has been canceled, so I hope to get some Xmas shopping done before I work my aft. noon shift.

_____

_____

Chapter 42   Exercise A
Numbers

In the space provided below each sentence, correct any numbers that are not treated according to the conventions for nonscientific writing.

1. Including taxes, the price came to nine thousand five hundred twenty dollars and thirty-four cents.

     _____

2. My office number is two thirty-four; I'm usually there and working at the computer by nine a.m.

     _____

3. In eighteen hundred cc of nitrogen, we dissolved three hundred fifty-four point nine gm of liquid sodium.

     _____

4. Physics one twenty-five meets on Thursday mornings.

     _____

5. On page six, the author cites a 12 percent increase in revenues for fiscal year nineteen hundred seventy-one.

     _____

6. The experiment began at six-oh-six; 15 cc were added to the solution every 5 minutes.

     _____

Chapter 42   Exercise B
Numbers

In the space provided below each sentence, correct any numbers that are not treated according to the conventions for nonscientific writing.

1. Lindsay moved from twelve Sycamore Lane to Sixteen-B Windsor Road, just past Interstate Seventy-Five.

_____

2. On June eight, nineteen hundred eighty-five, I made my final tuition payment of five hundred forty-seven dollars.

_____

3. Dinner will be served about 7.

_____

4. Breakfast ends at exactly nine a.m.

_____

5. Of the 619 names on the mailing list, 309 submitted the questionnaire by the deadline (which was March nine, 1998), but only twenty-two responded to every question.

_____

6. The restaurant is at 77 17th Avenue; I'll plan to meet you there no later than 1 o'clock on April sixth, 1990.

_____

Review Exercise A for Chapters 37-42
Spelling and Mechanics

Read the following sentences, looking for errors in spelling, capitalization, and hyphenation, and for misuse of italics, abbreviations, and numbers. In the space provided, write corrected forms of the following sentences.

1. After Mr Campbell asked for a dozen workers to assist with the Craft Fair at the nursing home, over 30 members of boy scout troop 172 volunteered because they enjoyed working with the residents at last year's event.

_____

_____

_____

_____

2. The scouts also know that mr campbell will reward them by cooking his specialty—Turkey and dressing dinner—on the next camping trip.

_____

_____

_____

3. The 3 wk unit of study culminated with Mr Hansard's dramatic
   reading of tennyson's famous poem, *The Charge of the Light
   Brigade*, accompanied by the overture from the Rossini's opera,
   William Tell.

   _____

   _____

   _____

   _____

4. When Mr Estabrook announced the expenses for last month's
   camporee (sixty five thousand eight hundred and fifty dollars), Mr
   Flerchinger was so startled that he almost fell out of his chair.

   _____

   _____

   _____

   _____

Name _____ Date _____ Score _____

Review Exercise B for Chapters 37-42
Spelling and Mechanics

Read the following sentences, looking for errors in spelling, capitalization, and hyphenation, and for misuse of italics, abbreviations, and numbers. In the space provided, write corrected forms of the following sentences.

1. Although the calendar said January, it was a surprisingly warm, spring like thurs. morning—January 28th, to be exact—and all andrew could think about was how he would celebrate his birthday with his brothers.

   _____

   _____

   _____

   _____

2. Luke earned a four year scholarship to the Fla. public college of his choice; his goal is to earn an m.a. & then choose a grad. school where he can earn a Doctorate.

   _____

   _____

   _____

Harcourt, Inc.

3. One of the most famous of eighteenth century literary pieces is Jonathan swift's gulliver's travels, which we read in our English Two-Eighteen class last semester.

4. The local teachers' union negotiated an excellent contract; each teacher will have twenty seven paid holidays—including two weeks during the christmas break; one week for the easter break; and her birthday, plus the day before and the day after.

Appendix A   Exercise A
Parts of Speech

Underline the nouns in the following sentences.

Example: Most <u>students</u> go to the weekly <u>dances</u>.

1.   In spite of the terrible downpour, 107,000 fans attended the game and stayed until the final buzzer.

2.   At the lake last summer, we fished each morning, swam each afternoon, and hiked each evening.

3.   The campus bookstore will be open late on Tuesday night, but it will close early on Friday afternoon.

4.   The University of North Carolina, located in the town of Chapel Hill, has buildings that date back to colonial days.

5.   The fencing team is a small group of dedicated athletes.

6.   The newspaper comes out every week and is noted for its lively articles and controversial columns.

7.   The crew of the lunar module performed the scheduled tasks and experiments before returning to base.

8.   Math exams can be especially challenging for students whose majors are in the humanities.

9.   Neil Armstrong was the first person to walk on the moon.

10. Chicken with mashed potatoes is my favorite meal.

Appendix A   Exercise B
Parts of Speech

Underline the correct pronoun in each sentence.

Example: Amy and (<u>she</u> / her) have excellent study habits.

1.   They pushed Adam and (I / me) down the hill.
2.   The sisters raced to (her / their) treehouse.
3.   The Risers and (we / us) plan to camp this weekend.
4.   The team's trophy is for (its / its) outstanding sportsmanship.
5.   Wanda and (I / me) will give our reports today.
6.   (Who / Whom) was looking for me this morning?
7.   (Who / Whom) did you meet at the airport?
8.   To (who / whom) did you address the letter?
9.   The new employees, Beth and (I / me), began the training program immediately.
10. The company's training program was designed for the new employees, Beth and (I / me).
11. Many of (we / us) students take classes and hold jobs.
12. (Him / He) and Margaret made a detailed map of the area.
13. Between you and (I / me), the new boss is great.
14. Jim knows more about zoology than (she / her).
15. Our supervisor encourages Sarah more than (I / me).

Appendix A   Exercise C
Parts of Speech

Underline the correct pronoun in each sentence.

1. They suspected that the prankster was (he / him).

2. I would not want to be (she / her).

3. Neither the general nor the soldier lost (his / their) life.

4. All of us have to do (her / our) jobs in this organization.

5. I left my coat with Fay and (they / them).

6. (We / Us) athletes all went out for the team.

7. My sister and (they / them) are good friends.

8. Who sent this package to (me / myself)?

9. All that confusion was caused by (him / himself).

10. I wish I were as easygoing as (they / themselves).

11. (He and I / Him and me) prefer to listen to classical music.

12. Neither Trish nor Kathy missed (her / their) class.

13. Eight of the plants produced (its / their) flowers as expected.

14. (Who / Whom) is the candidate of your choice?

15. For (who / whom) will you cast your vote?

Appendix A   Exercise D
Parts of Speech

Underline the nouns and pronouns that are examples of the case specified in parentheses for each sentence.

Example: (nominative or subjective) The <u>cat</u> ate the canary.

1. (nominative or subjective) The doctor is the speaker who will appear first.

2. (possessive) Our cat lay on my mother's bed and licked the boy's chewing gum from its paw.

3. (objective) Whom did you invite to the party?

4. (nominative or subjective) We will go there tomorrow.

5. (possessive) The governor's speech astounded many members of his audience.

6. (objective) Give it to them or they'll complain to me.

7. (nominative or subjective) She is as serious as he.

8. (possessive) The police asked whose purse was missing.

9. (nominative or subjective) The brothers, Allen and Gene, live in different states.

10. (possessive) His swimming at noon is a daily ritual.

11. (objective) I sat behind him and her.

12. (possessive) His coat is in their hall closet.

13. (possessive) Dr. Edmundson's lectures are packed with interesting stories.

14. (nominative or subjective) They can't walk far at this hour and in this weather.

Appendix A   Exercise E
Parts of Speech

In the space provided write "C" if the sentence is correct as it stands or "X" if it contains an error in possessive form. Circle and correct the incorrect form.

1. _____   In this group of students, their the innovators.

2. _____   They're opinion is considered important here.

3. _____   Whose the group that presented the asteroid project that

won first place in the contest?

4. _____   Who's turn is it to feed the piranha?

5. _____   The womens' softball team has been undefeated in the last

four tournaments in which it has competed.

Name _____ Date _____ Score _____

Appendix A   Exercise F
Parts of Speech

In the space provided, write "C" if the example has a complete verb or "I" if it has an incomplete verb.

1. _____ Brian and Beth visited Yosemite National Park.

2. _____ All members of the Beta Club to attend the baseball game.

3. _____ Scouts with flashlights served as guides along the path.

4. _____ What the surgeon told the class of interns.

5. _____ My computer has crashed only once this week.

6. _____ Crashed or froze ten times last week.

7. _____ Most students prefer to purchase used textbooks.

8. _____ Everybody to hurry for shelter.

9. _____ With friends they enjoying the snow.

10. _____ Mike and Diane making snowballs.

11. _____ The wind blowing and chilling.

12. _____ A blizzard might have been coming.

13. _____ Errands to the bank, the post office, and the bakery.

14. _____ Why are all research papers due just before Thanksgiving?

15. _____ The rain in Spain mainly on the plain.

Appendix A   Exercise G
Parts of Speech

Complete each sentence by underlining the appropriate form of the verb in parentheses.

Example: The fisherman (<u>caught</u> / was caught by) the trout.

1. The attorney (reviewed / was reviewed by) the contracts.

2. The dog (combed / was combed by) its trainer.

3. The professor (graded / was graded by) the essays.

4. The church bell (rang / was rung by) the elderly caretaker.

5. The hungry loggers (ate / were eaten by) the pancakes.

6. The pancakes (ate / were eaten by) the hungry loggers.

7. The prize cucumber (grew / was grown by) Cathy Cowart.

8. Amanda (answered / was answered by) every question in the review section at the end of the chapter.

9. Each e-mail submission to the contest (answers / is answered by) the computer, which sends an acknowledgement by return e-mail.

10. When a caller leaves a message, it (records / is recorded by) the answering machine.

11. Occasionally the tape (skips / is skipped by) a message.

12. The cat (has untangled / has been untangled by) the ball of twine.

Harcourt, Inc.

Appendix A   Exercise H
Parts of Speech

Underline the correct adjective in each sentence.

1. Sarah's hair is naturally (curled / curly).

2. In two pages, write (a / an) history of American film.

3. Brenda looks (tired / tiredly).

4. Reece wears only (sloppy / sloppily) clothes.

5. What an (unsightly / unsighted) mess!

6. Ronnie waited for this (luckily / lucky) break.

7. Caitlin combed her (gold / golden) hair.

8. The strawberry jam is too (sweet / sweetly).

9. Laura stopped at (their / theirs) apartment yesterday.

10. (Each / Both) sheep are ready for shearing.

11. (Each / Both) sheep has its own pedigree.

12. (This / These) crew will report for duty tomorrow.

13. (This / These) crew members are on vacation.

14. The movie had one (tense / tenser) moment after another.

15. Negotiators avoided (a / an) union strike.

Appendix A   Exercise I
Parts of Speech

Underline the adjectives in the following sentences.

1. The staff worked best with a definite deadline.

2. Jessie grabbed her old boots and ran hurriedly.

3. The six dogs ran ahead, playfully romping in the high grass.

4. The trip is rather long, but we usually arrive in two days.

5. We anxiously awaited Mother's call to eat the delicious meal that she had meticulously placed on a beautifully decorated table.

6. Diane carelessly left her blue backpack in the classroom.

7. Very soon the cold water began dripping loudly on the parquet floor in the vacant room.

8. Joel may be quite tall, but he has never played basketball.

9. From their dazed appearance, we concluded that each exhausted hiker was ready for a warm bath, a bowl of hot soup, and a long rest in a cozy bed.

10. In the final competition, the group of four students worked amazingly well together as they addressed each perplexing task that the committee presented.

Name _____ Date _____ Score _____

Appendix A   Exercise J
Parts of Speech

Underline the correct adverb in each sentence.

1. To close the window, turn the crank (gentle / gently).

2. Raise the garage door as (careful / carefully) as possible.

3. Even in the worst weather, Trish is (seldom / seldomly) late.

4. Weeks of practice paid off when the play was executed (perfect / perfectly) and Beth's team won the game in the final seconds.

5. Don fought (manly / manfully) for his rights.

6. Fay could (usual / usually) run quickly.

7. Erica (rare / rarely) displays anger on the field.

8. Everyone thought (high / highly) of Coach Cowart.

9. Loose gravel convinced them to ride (slow / slowly) on their bikes.

10. In spite of the muddy track, the horse raced (fast / fastly).

11. I enjoy watching the camels running (graceful / gracefully).

12. The children ran (wild / wildly) across the playground.

13. Cathy visited her mother (often / oftenly).

14. The bell rang (more loudly / most loudly) than ever.

15. The green team finished (last / lastly).

Appendix A   Exercise K
Parts of Speech

Underline the adverbs in the following sentences.

1. The staff worked best with a definite deadline.

2. Jessie grabbed her old boots and ran hurriedly.

3. Julie actually knew she would do well on the exam.

4. The dog's heart beat loudly as he panted rapidly.

5. Camille's extremely regal appearance surprised her friends.

6. We sometimes review customer accounts randomly.

7. The six dogs ran ahead, playfully romping in the high grass.

8. Stomach pains are most often caused by overeating.

9. They danced gracefully despite the band's mistakes.

10. The trip is rather long, but we usually arrive in two days.

11. We anxiously awaited Mother's call to eat the delicious meal that
    she had meticulously placed on a beautifully decorated table.

12. Diane carelessly left her blue backpack in the classroom.

13. Very soon the cold water began dripping loudly on the parquet
    floor in the vacant room.

14. Joel may be quite tall, but he has never played basketball.

15. Claire is unlikely to be home now; try again tomorrow.

Appendix A   Exercise L
Parts of Speech

For each sentence, underline the most logical of the prepositions in parentheses.

1. The balloon descended (above / around / to) the ground.

2. The ten children got along well (in spite of / by way of / between) their age differences.

3. As the children watched helplessly, the ball rolled (with / across / on account of) the concrete driveway.

4. To everyone's amazement, the magician waved his wand and then lofted the rabbit (beyond / in back of / above) his head.

5. (After / Before / Between) the storm left the area, the sky darkened, thunder rumbled, and the rain came down in buckets.

6. (Among / Between / In spite of) you and me, I think this will be an action-packed spring break.

7. At night during the summer months, the city lights cast a spooky glow (within / up to / behind) the dark hill.

8. To the dismay of the judge, the news spread rapidly (between / among / through) the jury members.

9. The monster growled and crept slowly (to / toward / regarding) the cowering heroine.

10. In our neighborhood, the Sunday newspaper always arrives (until / during / before) 8:15 A.M.

Appendix A   Exercise M
Parts of Speech

Underline the prepositions in the following sentences.

1. At the beginning of the term, the bookstore is not an enjoyable place to visit because it is too crowded.

2. Despite being excited about new courses, students are needlessly exhausted by the lines at the bookstore.

3. All the books are arranged under the names of the departments, so I had to make several stops to find mine.

4. When other students blocked the aisles, I had to push by to get to the right place to find my books.

5. The books for my English course were on the top shelf.

6. To get them, I had to climb up on a ladder that was shaking because of the jostling crowd.

7. My fear of heights, however, was less than my fear of being trampled when I found my math books on the bottom shelf, behind those for calculus.

8. After my books were gathered up, I saw that the lines for the cashiers wound behind the sweatshirts and in front of the dictionaries.

9. I stood in line for an hour, thumbing through my books and talking with other students during the wait.

10. At last I had my books and was ready to practice my weight lifting on the long walk back to my room.

11. My mom thinks I'm too much of a complainer, but what does she know about life at college?

Appendix A   Exercise N
Parts of Speech

Complete the sentences below by filling in the most logical prepositions from the following list.

against	at	during	in	into
of	on	under	with	

Example: The Gunpowder Plot occurred _on_____
            November 5, 1605.

1. _____ that time of religious strife, King James I ruled England, a Protestant country.

2. _____ November 5, he was to open Parliament with a formal ceremony.

3. The plan of the Catholic conspirators was to blow up Parliament _____that time.

4. Then they expected their fellow English Catholics to rise up _____ the Protestant government that suppressed their religion.

5. To carry out their plot, the conspirators had rented a cellar _____ Westminster, where the House of Lords met.

6. There they had stored thirty-six kegs of gunpowder, covered _____ firewood and coal.

7. Some members _____ the House of Lords received warning letters, urging them not to attend.

8. The secret cellar was discovered, and one conspirator, Guy Fawkes, was arrested when he came _____ the cellar.

9. _____ England, November 5 is still called Guy Fawkes Day.

10. _____ that day, fireworks and bonfires commemorate the discovery of the plot.

Appendix A Exercise O
Parts of Speech

Underline the conjunctions in the following sentences.

Example: They were so hungry that they ate <u>not</u> <u>only</u>
            the eggs and sausage <u>but</u> <u>also</u> the doughnuts
            <u>and</u> coffeecake.

1. Both Carol and Doug enjoy the circus clowns.

2. Either Don will buy the clock, or he will pass up a great offer.

3. Staci and Linda had to wait in the hall until the doors opened.

4. We did our best, whatever happens next.

5. Normally the course has a prerequisite; nevertheless, the professor
    may admit a student without it.

6. Unless Beth leaves now, she will miss the return flight.

7. The lectures are twice a week; in addition, students must attend
    weekly labs and discussion groups.

8. Erica selected the college because it has a fine reputation.

9. Neither her mother nor her father expected her to call.

10. Morning came, yet the sky remained gray.

11. Call the fire department or the ambulance squad.

12. The police officer assured me that the burglar alarm would continue
    to ring unless someone turns it off.

Name _____ Date _____ Score _____

Appendix A   Exercise P
Parts of Speech

Underline the correct conjunction in each sentence.

Example: She eats constantly (and / <u>but</u>) remains thin.

1. (Since / Because) the school was founded, it has offered courses in theology and ethics.

2. The department of religion (and / but) philosophy offers both courses each semester.

3. (While / Once) you wait for your interview, you might want to review the job requirements.

4. I had to take the 8 a.m. section (because / although) that was the only vacant slot in my schedule.

5. She knew when the paper was due; (consequently / nevertheless), she handed it in a week late.

6. He wanted to take a course in nearly every department; (moreover / for example), he thought everyone should read Shakespeare, study philosophy, and review American history.

7. Look in the dining hall (or / but) in the lounge.

8. Neither the regular fire drills (nor / but also) the occasional false alarms had prepared the students for the trauma of the real fire that struck their dorm that stormy winter night.

9. The crocuses were blooming (although / before) snow still covered the ground.

10. The baby refuses to eat (lest / unless) her grandmother feeds her.

Appendix A   Exercise Q
Parts of Speech

Use the conjunctions in parentheses to link the following short sentences or fragments. Rewrite and punctuate as necessary to generate a sentence that is smooth and correct.

Example: You should hurry. We are going to be late. (unless)

Unless you hurry, we are going to be late.

1.   The program aired. The executives had debated whether to release it. (before)

_____

2.   The dining hall serves three meals a day. Students must eat during the serving hours. (however)

_____

_____

3.   The western cowboy. The frontiersman. Blend truth with American mythology. (both, and)

_____

4.   The administrators. The faculty. Correctly projected enrollment trends. (neither, nor)

_____

Appendix A   Exercise R
Parts of Speech

Underline the interjections in the following sentences.

1. Wow! Can you imagine how excited Beth was?

2. From the examination room, I heard someone yell, "Ouch!"

    There's no way I'm staying here. I'll see you at home.

3. When I ask Grandma, she always says, "Oh, you're just like your

    father when he was your age."

4. When the mouse ran through the garage, Aunt Alice shouted,

    "Heavens!" and then grabbed the broom.

Name _____ Date _____ Score _____

Appendix B   Exercise A
Sentence Review

In the space provided, write "S" if the example has a subject or "X" if it does not. Underline the simple subjects that you find.

Example: __S__ Everyone liked my new car.

1. _____ More than you will ever know.

2. _____ Forty chairs per classroom.

3. _____ Need several pounds of shrimp.

4. _____ We played cards until after midnight

5. _____ Meg cares about her patients

6. _____ Comprehension and vocabulary.

7. _____ Beyond his limit, Brian took a break.

8. _____ Is running several miles each morning.

9. _____ Love going to the mall.

10. _____ Our vacation was refreshing.

Appendix B   Exercise B
Sentence Review

On your own paper, expand each basic sentence by adding at least a phrase or a clause.

Example: George bought a car.
            George bought a car that he will pick up Monday.

1. The dog barked.

2. Sarah bought a house.

3. I will finish my homework.

4. The food is cooked.

5. The doctor will be back Tuesday.

6. Stop the red car.

7. My brother called.

8. The dean spoke.

9. We began our vacation.

10. My cousin is a lawyer.

11. I rode the trolley.

12. When do you leave?

13. The library is closed.

14. He swam a dozen laps.

15. He played the violin.

Appendix B   Exercise C
Sentence Review

For each of the following sentences, identify the basic sentence pattern. Ignore any added modifiers, phrases, or dependent clauses. Identify the pattern using these abbreviations:

s + v (subject + intransitive verb)

s + v + do (subject + transitive verb + direct object)

s + v + io + do (subject + transitive verb + indirect object + direct object)

s + v + do + oc (subject + transitive verb + direct object + object complement)

s + v + sc (subject + linking verb + subject complement— predicate noun or adjective)

Example:

___S + V + IO + DO_____ The mayor pitched Robin the first ball of the season.

1. _____ The cardinals built their nest.

2. _____ The birds fed their babies the worms.

3. _____ The canals on Mars resemble an irrigation system.

4. _____ The class elected Frank.

5. _____ The class elected Frank president.

Harcourt, Inc.

Appendix B   Exercise D
Sentence Review

For each of the following sentences, identify the basic sentence pattern. Ignore any added modifiers, phrases, or dependent clauses. Identify the pattern using these abbreviations:

s + v (subject + intransitive verb)

s + v + do (subject + transitive verb + direct object)

s + v + io + do (subject + transitive verb +
                        indirect object + direct object)

s + v + do + oc (subject + transitive verb +
                        direct object + object complement)

s + v + sc (subject + linking verb + subject complement—
               predicate noun or adjective)

Example:

___S + V + IO + DO____ The mayor pitched Robin the first ball of the season.

1. _____ That solar system disintegrated.

2. _____ The solar system disintegrated years ago.

3. _____ The exam was difficult.

4. _____ The soccer team won.

5. _____ The soccer team won the championship yesterday.

6. _____ The soccer team became the champions.

Appendix C   Exercise A
Language Issues for International Students

No pronouns are present in the following passage. The repetition of the nouns would seem strange to a native speaker of English. On your own paper, rewrite the passage, replacing as many of the nouns as possible with appropriate pronouns. Be sure that the connection between the pronoun and the noun it replaces is clear.

The young couple seated across from Daniel at the dinner the night before were newlyweds from Tokyo. The young couple and Daniel ate together with other guests of the inn at long, low tables in a large dining room. The man introduced himself immediately in English, shook Daniel's hand firmly, and, after learning that Daniel was not a tourist but a resident working in Osaka, gave Daniel a business card. The man had just finished college and was working at the man's first real job, clerking in a bank. Even in a sweatsuit, the man looked ready for the office: chin closely shaven, bristly hair neatly clipped, nails clean and buffed. After a while, the man and Daniel exhausted the man's store of English and drifted into Japanese.

The man's wife, shy up until then, took over as the man fell silent. The woman and Daniel talked about the new popularity of hot springs spas in the countryside around the inn, the difficulty of finding good schools for the children the woman hoped to have soon, and the differences between food in Tokyo and Osaka. The woman's husband ate busily with an air of tolerating the woman's prattling. From time to time, the woman refilled the man's beer glass to served the man radish pickles from a china bowl in the middle of the table, and then returned to the conversation.

Appendix C   Exercise B
Language Issues for International Students

In the following passage, identify all the infinitives (*to* _____),
gerunds (_____*ing*), present participles (_____*ing*), and
past participles (_____ed, _____t, or _____en).
Define the function of each as either noun or adjective.

The car is the quintessential American possession. The car, not the

home, is the center of American life. Despite its central place in the

mystique of the American Dream, the individually owned home is

actually anti-American in many ways. Owning a car means freedom,

progress, and individual initiative, the most basic American values. To

own a house means rusting pipes and rotting roof beams. Staying in

one place implies stagnation and decay, whereas moving (always

"forward") connotes energy, creativity, never-ending youth: "Moss

doesn't grow on a rolling stone." And the way Americans move is in

their cars, their personalized, self-contained, mobile units.

Appendix C   Exercise C
Language Issues for International Students

Each sentence below is followed by a list of adjectives and adverbs that can be used in the sentence. Place the adjectives and adverbs where they belong in each sentence. Adjectives and adverbs are listed in the order in which they should appear in the sentences.

1. Researchers believe that tests are not reliable.

    (most, now, IQ, entirely)

    _____

2. Just as culture is derived from Greece, culture is derived from China. (European, ancient, Asian, ancient)

    _____

    _____

3. The people of Louisiana play a music called zydeco.

    (Cajun, southern, lively)

    _____

4. According to the Japanese proverb, for a lid there's a pot.

    (old, cracked, chipped)

    _____

Harcourt, Inc.

Appendix C   Exercise D
Language Issues for International Students

Each sentence below is followed by a list of adjectives and adverbs that can be used in the sentence. Place the adjectives and adverbs where they belong in each sentence. Adjectives and adverbs are listed in the order in which they should appear in the sentences.

1. Because I transferred credits from my school, I was able to graduate. (many, previous, early)

    _____

    _____

2. Often, feminists feel they are describing the condition of women in the world, when they are describing women in America.

    (too, American, all, actually, only)

    _____

    _____

3. Kenjy works hours on essays, but he remembers to take breaks.

    (usually, many, periodic)

    _____

4. When you begin to exercise, start and build up to levels.

    (slowly, steadily, strenuous)

    _____

Answers to Selected Exercises

Chapter 1   Exercise B (p. 2)
Determining Your Purpose

Answers will vary. Choose a subject that can be developed into the first essay of the term.

Chapter 1   Exercise D (p. 4)
Freewriting

Answers will vary.

Chapter 1   Exercise F (p. 6)
Journal Entry

Answers will vary.

Chapter 1   Exercise H (p. 8)
Developing a Thesis

1. An announcement, not a thesis.
1. A subject, not a thesis. Gives no indication of essay's focus or direction; nor does it mention writer's position.
1. A subject, not a thesis. Why should it be avoided? What coast? What kind of development? What constitutes overdevelopment?
1. No position indicated. What aspects will be considered? What pattern of development might be used? What standards of judgment will be used?
1. A good start, although "but it has some disadvantages" is not sufficiently specific.
1. A subject, not a thesis. What position? Do all environmentalists share a single position?
1. States a fact.
1. A good start, but needs clearer focus. Thesis is too general.
1. States a fact.
1. States a personal opinion. Question of taste. Hard to develop objectively or concretely.

Chapter 1   Exercise J (p. 10)
Stating a Thesis

Answers will vary.

Chapter 1   Exercise L (p. 12)
Rough Draft

Answers will vary.

Chapter 1   Exercise N (p. 14)
Customized Checklist

Answers will vary.

Chapter 1   Exercise P (p. 16)
Central Idea—Topic Sentence

Answers will vary.
Unifying idea: Themes of Ralph Ellison's novel *Invisible Man*
Topic sentence: In *Invisible Man*, Ralph Ellison is concerned at least as much with self-discovery as he is with race relations. (This sentence could be placed at either the beginning or the end of the paragraph.)

Chapter 2   Exercise B (p.18)
Coherence within Paragraphs

The theory of continental drift was first put forward by Alfred Wegener in 1912. *He believed that* the continents fit together like a gigantic jigsaw puzzle. *Because* the opposing Atlantic coasts, especially South America and Africa, seem to have been attached, *he also believed that* at one time, probably 225 million years ago, there was one supercontinent *which* broke into parts that drifted into their present positions. The theory*, which* stirred controversy during the 1920s, eventually was ridiculed by the scientific community. *However, the theory of continental drift was revived* in 1954 *and* is accepted as a reasonable geological explanation of the continental system.

Chapter 2   Exercise D (p. 20)
Patterns of Paragraph Development

Answers will vary.

1. cause and effect, classification, narration
2. cause and effect, narration, process analysis
3. classification, description, exemplification
4. cause and effect, classification, comparison and contrast
5. definition, description, exemplification
6. argumentation, classification, exemplification
7. cause and effect, exemplification, narration
8. argumentation, cause and effect, classification
9. argumentation, classification, exemplification
10. classification, exemplification

Chapter 2   Exercise F (p. 22)
Patterns of Paragraph Development

This paragraph could be further developed by enumeration of amounts
of specific ingredients, types of containers, and utensils used. Baking
times and temperatures can vary. Methods of storing and preserving the
batter could be included. Flavoring and leavening are important
ingredients to be discussed. Generally accepted bread-making
procedures could be used as a guide for completing the process.

Review Exercise B for Chapters 1-2 (p. 24)
Writing Essays and Paragraphs

Answers will vary.
The paragraph could be developed by using process analysis. It is
important that the steps of the planning process are complete and in
order. Remember to include appropriate warnings that will guide the
reader to avoid issues that could undermine the effectiveness of the
gathering.

Chapter 3   Exercise B (p. 26)
Thinking Critically

1. F
2. O, statistics, expert testimony
3. O, statistics, expert testimony, examples
4. O, statistics, expert testimony, examples
5. O, statistics
6. F

Chapter 4   Exercise B (p. 28)
Writing Argumentative Essays

Answers will vary.

Review Exercise B for Chapters 3-4 (p. 31)
Critical Thinking and Argumentation

Answers will vary. A possible revision follows.

Television Violence: Let Us Exercise Our Choice

Television began as what many people thought was a fad. Now, over fifty years later, it is the subject of arguments and controversy. As a result, numerous activist groups have formed with the intent to examine television's role in society. Some such groups are devoted entirely to protesting against violence on television. However, what these groups fail to recognize is that banning television violence is a form of censorship that does more harm than good.

As one examines censorship of violence on television, it is important to remember that the broadcast industry is a business. Success in business is most obviously achieved by meeting the demands of the customer. In the case of television, the viewers are the customers, and many express the desire for realism in television programming.

Additionally, the First Amendment of the United States Constitution guarantees all citizens the right of free speech. In part, the first amendment is a reflection of the concept that an informed citizenry is the best defense against tyranny. An examination of other countries such as Iran and China, where the people see only what the government wants them to see, provides examples of censorship at its most extreme. Although censoring violence on television would not necessarily result in a complete loss of our freedoms, it might well open the door to more far-reaching forms of censorship in the future.

Although television reflects the violence in American society, it does not create violence. Obviously, other factors in society—such as drugs, the proliferation of guns, and increased unemployment—contribute to the increase in violence in America. Only by being aware of these problems, in part through the realism of television, can we acknowledge them and begin to work toward resolving the issues.

Even though there are no simple solutions to the problem of violence in American, television censorship of violence is not the answer. Such censorship would only result in the absence of realism and would blind Americans to the ills in our society that have led to violence in the first place. Because television is a powerful medium, perhaps we should examine ways to expand its influence to help us recognize our problems and find solutions to them rather than shackling programming with censorship.

Chapter 5   Exercise B (p. 34)
Discovering Your Research Question

Answers will vary.

Chapter 5   Exercise D (p. 36)
Discovering Your Research Question

Answers will vary.

Chapter 6   Exercise B (p. 38)
Exploring Your Topic and Locating Sources

Answers will vary.

Chapter 6   Exercise D (p. 40)
Evaluating Sources

Answers will vary.

Chapter 7   Exercise B (p. 42)
Locating and Evaluating Sources on the Web Using a Key Word
Search

Answers will vary.

Chapter 7   Exercise D (p. 44)
Citing Electronic Sources

Answers will vary. Refer to the Documentation section in *The Brief
Holt Handbook*.

Chapter 8   Exercise B (p. 46)
Integrating Sources and Avoiding Plagiarism

Answers will vary. One sample follows.

    To accommodate these people, homebuilders turned farmlands
into developments of three-bedroom houses owned by young couples
holding government loans. By 1960, the percentage of homeowners had
risen above that of renters; most homeowners now lived in the new
suburbs.

Chapter 8   Exercise D (p. 48)
Paraphrase

Answers will vary. One sample follows.

    The suburbs became "gigantic nurseries." Abraham Levitt, the
son of Russian-Jewish immigrants and the builder of military barracks
in World War II, constructed the largest developments. A Long Island
potato field became the first Levittown, which housed 82,000 people in
17,447 homes. Two more communities were built on the East Coast.

Each offered identical four-room houses with built-in television, outdoor grill, washer, and attic for $7,900, or $60 per month. The common denominator among Levittown residents was the desire to have children.

Chapter 8   Exercise F (p. 50)
Documentation

1.   Parenthetical citations
Answers will vary.

2.   Works Cited entry
Jones, Landon Y. *Great Expectations: America and the Baby Boom Generation.* New York: Ballantine, 1986.

Review Exercise B for Chapters 5-8 (p. 53)
Research

Answers will vary.

Chapter 9   Exercise B (p. 56)
MLA Documentation Format

Answers will vary.

Chapter 10   Exercise B (p. 58)
APA and Other Documentation Formats

Answers will vary.

Review Exercise B for Chapters 9-10 (p. 60)
Survival Skills

1.   O'Neill, Terry. Introduction. Censorship: Opposing Viewpoints. St. Paul: Greenhaven, 1985. 13-14.

2.   Hentoff, Nat. "The Speech Police Invade Cyberspace." <u>Village Voice</u> 11 July 1995: 22-23.

Chapter 11   Exercise B (p. 62)
Developing Reading Skills

Answers will vary.

Chapter 12   Exercise B (p. 64)
Writing Essay Examinations

Answers will vary.

Chapter 13   Exercise B (p. 66)
Writing about Literature

Answers will vary.

Chapter 14   Exercise B (p. 68)
Document Design and Manuscript Format

Answers will vary.

Chapter 15   Exercise B (p. 7I)
Writing for the Workplace

Answers will vary.

Review Exercise B for Chapters 11-15 (p. 74)
Academic and Professional Survival Skills

Answers will vary.

Chapter 16   Exercise B (p. 76)
Revising Sentence Fragments

When we moved from an apartment to a house, we discovered that we had more belongings than we thought. So much had to be packed, so we used boxes, suitcases, and even large garbage bags. We rented a truck from the local gas station so we could avoid spending the extra money to hire a mover. We certainly put in a full day's work that day. Although the process was long and hard, it was worth it.

Chapter 16   Exercise D (p. 78)
Revising Sentence Fragments

1. Because the officials did not like the thunder that shook the ground and lightning that brightened the sky, the soccer tournament was postponed until Saturday.
2. Erica not only struck out eleven batters, but she also hit two doubles and drove in five runs.
3. Neither the administrators nor the faculty correctly projected enrollment trends.

Chapter 17   Exercise B (p. 80)
Revising Comma Splices and Fused Sentences

1. RO	speak / the		6. RO	players / Reece
2. RO	letter / another		7. RO	deck / his
3. RO	business / everyone		8. RO	call / has
4. RO	small / only		9. RO	detail / each
5. C			10. RO	you / I

Chapter 17   Exercise D (p. 82)
Revising Comma Splices and Fused Sentences

Cats make great pets, but you have to be affectionate with them. As they are rather independent animals, they do not always come when you call them. Many people prefer dogs because you can train them to come or sit or fetch a bone. With cats, on the other hand, you have to be willing to let them live their own lives. If you attempt to train them, you may become discouraged. If you put two cats in the same room, you are in for quite a treat. They chase each other, usually all in fun. When one catches the other, the real show begins. Often they will cuddle and clean each other, but sometimes they will fight. The wise pet owner will know when to break up a fight and when to let it go, because it is only play for the cats. They can be great company if you understand them.

Chapter 18   Exercise B (p. 84)
Revising Agreement Errors

1. The subject *he* (singular) agrees with the verb *fishes*;
2. the subject Mr. Mims (singular although it ends in *s*) agrees with the verb *comes*;
3. the subject *he* (singular) agrees with the verb *considers*.
4. *Every* (singular) serves as the subject for the verb *was;*
5. the subject *thunderstorm* agrees with the verb *passed.*
6. The subject *Aerodynamics* (singular although it ends in *s*) agrees with the verb *is.*

Chapter 18   Exercise D (p. 86)
Revising Agreement Errors

Carpenters use many different tools in their work. When they are faced with jobs that are particularly difficult, they have to use their patience as well as their skills. Without patience, hammers, saws, or screwdrivers will do carpenters no good. They have to be able to understand the problems, and find the best ways to solve them. Sometimes, the quickest solutions are not the best. Their customers, or clients, have to be pleased with their work, or they lose their chances to be hired for other jobs. There are great pressures on carpenters to succeed. By no means are their jobs easy.

Chapter 18   Exercise F (p. 88)
Revising Agreement Errors

1. their
2. his
3. its
4. her
5. its

6. its
7. his
8. his
9. his
10. their

Chapter 19   Exercise B (p. 90)
Revising Awkward or Confusing Sentences

1. close; need
   closed, needed
2. wants; hates
   wanted; hated
3. stay; pay
   stayed; paid
4. washed; began
   washes; begin
5. runs; hopes
   ran; hoped

Chapter 19   Exercise D (p. 92)
Revising Awkward or Confusing Sentences

      I work in a bank, and when one has that type of job, he has to be willing to wake up at a very early hour. Each morning, I drive to work, park my car, and walked a block to work. I get a lunch break every day at noon, and I love to eat at the delicatessen around the corner. I worked at the bank for over a year, and decided that I had had enough. After looking around for a new job, I found one where I had to be at work at 6:00 a.m. This job was in a restaurant where I had to stand up all day, and after six months, I decided to go back to the bank. The manager was very nice to me and said, "You can have your old job back if you promise to stay at least two years." I take the job, and I enjoy an extra hour of sleep every morning.

Chapter 20 Exercise B (p. 94)
Revising Misplaced and Dangling Modifiers

1. Although a small part of the world's population, people in developed countries are using up proportionally more of the earth's nonrenewable natural resources.
2. As fossil fuels, minerals, metals, timber, and water are diminishing, they cannot be replaced because they were built up over billions of years.
3. With the doubling of the world consumption of oil every decade, time would seem short for a change.
4. When certain coastal areas are flooded, such minerals as common salt, magnesium, and bromine can be extracted from seawater through evaporation.
5. According to experts, one-half to one-third of the world's additional energy needs in the next twenty years will be satisfied by the use of coal, although it pollutes the atmosphere.

Chapter 20 Exercise D (p. 96)
Revising Misplaced and Dangling Modifiers

On arriving in America, Pierre was amazed by the sights and sounds. Because he traveled alone, the sight of so many people hurrying around and shouting came as a jolt to him. Coming from a small village in the south of France, the young traveler had never before witnessed so much commotion. He was only eight years old and a bit nervous, and his luggage seemed to be his only companion. On this trip, his cousins in Philadelphia would be his hosts. Looking for them at the gate, he was not able to find them. Then an attendant took him to the information booth and paged his cousins over the loudspeaker. To locate them, the attendant had to make an announcement twice. Then Pierre recognized his relatives running through the terminal, from the other end of the building. Feeling relieved, Pierre ran to them and escaped the crazy crowds of America.

228

Making Waffles

After a long night's sleep, how would you like to sit down to a cup of hot coffee and golden brown waffles for breakfast? You would probably like them with warm strawberries and a scoop of fresh, whipped cream, or you might prefer the traditional butter and maple syrup. In any case, waffles are an excellent breakfast dish, for they are easy to prepare, and there are many ways to serve them. Basically, making waffles involves three steps: preparing the batter, cooking the waffle, and deciding how to top it.

First, before mixing the batter, it is a good idea to preheat the waffle iron. Most irons have to be plugged in, and usually take from ten to fifteen minutes to heat up. I have found that medium is usually the best setting, but you'll have to decide which setting works best for you.

Mixing the batter is a relatively simple task. First, combine the following in a large mixing bowl: one cup cake flour, two tablespoons of sugar, two teaspoons of baking powder, and one-fourth teaspoon of salt.

Next, add one cup of milk and one tablespoon of vegetable oil to the dry ingredients. It is important to add the oil to the batter; otherwise, the waffles will stick to the iron. If you don't have any vegetable oil, one tablespoon of melted butter or margarine will suffice. Use a medium-sized spoon to stir the batter until it forms a smooth mixture without any lumps in it.

After thoroughly stirring the batter, making sure that there aren't any lumps in it, crack two eggs into a small bowl. Take care not to break the yolks, and make sure that there aren't any pieces of shell in the bowl.

Next, separate the yolks with a small spoon, and store them in an appropriate container, since they will not be added to the batter. Use a small fork to beat the egg whites until they become frothy. Then, combine the egg whites with the batter, mixing them in completely. Preparing the egg whites in this manner seems like a waste of time when you could just toss them into the batter. But this way, the waffles turn out with a light, fluffy texture on the inside.

By this time, the waffle iron is probably finished preheating. Use the mixing spoon to put some batter in the waffle iron, filling all of the ridges of the iron's bottom side. Now, use a low, medium, or high setting to cook the waffle to your desired preference, golden brown, or for some, burned. Following these instructions will produce four medium-sized waffles.

Finally, the hardest part of preparing waffles is deciding what topping to use. Whatever topping you decide to use—fruit and cream, butter and syrup, or even ice cream—waffles are always a special as well as a splendid addition to anyone's breakfast menu treat. Try them sometime.

Chapter 21   Exercise B (p. 103)
Using Verbs Correctly

1. moved
2. knit, sew
3. were
4. could light
5. sputter, flicker, drip
6. wrote
7. did write
8.will be responsible

9. should be used
10. will bring
11. visited
12 hopes
13. could have served
14. has crashed
15. would prefer
16. has been seen

Chapter 21   Exercise D (p. 105)
Using Verbs Correctly

1. escorted, to take, are waiting [or will wait]
2. began
3. had listened
4. sat
5. broke

Chapter 21   Exercise F (p. 107)
Using Verbs Correctly

The Regent Diamond is one of the world's most famous and coveted jewels. The 410-carat diamond was discovered by a slave in 1701 in an Indian mine. [Emphasis is on the diamond rather than on who discovered it.] Over the years, it was stolen and sold several times. [Emphasis is on what happened rather than on *people*.] In 1717, the Regent of France bought the diamond for an enormous sum, but during the French Revolution, it disappeared again. It was later discovered in a ditch in Paris. [Emphasis is on its eventual discovery rather than on who discovered it.] Eventually, Napoleon had the diamond set into his ceremonial sword. At last, when the French monarch fell, the Regent Diamond was placed in the Louvre, where it still remains to be enjoyed by all. [Emphasis is on where it was placed rather than on who placed it there.]

Chapter 22   Exercise B (p. 109)
Using Pronouns Correctly

Answers will vary.

Chapter 22   Exercise D (p. 111)
Using Pronouns Correctly

1. their
2. Whose
3. its
4. It's
5. your
6. their
7. Who's
8. governor's
9. Women's
10. your

Chapter 23   Exercise B (p. 113)
Using Adjectives and Adverbs Correctly

1. unique
2. more delicate
3. more sick
4. taller
5. heavier
6. heaviest
7. grateful
8. youngest
9. faster
10. worse

The following is one example of effective revision.

Dusty

On January 28, 1987, Dusty, my two-year-old Doberman pinscher, was born. Six months following his birth, I began to train Dusty with Mr. Wagner, a professional dog trainer. After two weeks of obedience training, Dusty learned the "Heel" and "Sit" commands. We worked for four more weeks, spending thirty minutes a day on more basic obedience commands. Dusty, of course, responds very well. Not only he learned all of the obedience commands, but he and I had also built a strong relationship. We were best friends.

During the final week of training, Mr. Wagner said that I had been more successful with Dusty that he had seen anybody else accomplish with a dog since he was in the training business. He said, "I am proud of the accomplishments that you and Dusty have made."

I felt good about what I had done with Dusty and how he had learned all of those obedience commands. Dusty and I continued to work with one another for a year. During that time he had taken on some behaviors that I had nothing to do with. For instance, he attacked anyone who threatened to harm any member of my family. If Dusty saw my parents or brothers hit me, Dusty attacked them. Should someone else hit a member of my family, Dusty attacked that person. If Dusty didn't recognize someone driving down our driveway, Dusty ran back and forth in front of the car to make the driver slow down before reaching our yard. He also didn't permit a stranger to take one step out of his car. Dusty became very well mannered and protective of us.

A year and a half later, a tragedy happened. One summer day, my father drove a different truck down our driveway. Dusty hadn't really recognized who was driving the truck or the truck itself, so he darted in front of the truck, trying to make it slow down before entering the yard. Unfortunately, the right front wheel hit Dusty in the hind leg, and the right back wheel hit him in the head.

Fortunately, Dusty was still alive! He didn't allow anyone but me to help him. Scared to death, I picked him up and put him in the back of the truck. My brother rushed Dusty and me to the animal hospital. Dusty's blood is all over my hands and shirt, but I didn't care. All I wanted was for Dusty to have the best medical care possible. Nearly crying, I lifted Dusty from the truck and took him inside the animal hospital.

After four days of treatment, the veterinarians allowed me to take Dusty home, provided that I kept him under close supervision. Limping away from the veterinarians, Dusty was eager to go home. Another two weeks passed before he had totally healed. After Dusty had recovered, we continued his training, and he has made even more astonishing accomplishments. I am so proud of Dusty! Now that I am in college, I miss him very much, but I will see him again when I go home.

Chapter 24   Exercise B (p. 119)
Writing Varied Sentences

A. One of the more intriguing literary legends surrounding the King James Version of the Bible alleges that Shakespeare's hand is present in the 46th Psalm.

B. Turn to the psalm to see for yourself.

A. Count to the forty-sixth word from the beginning of the psalm (*shake*) and then identify the forty-sixth word from the end of the psalm (*spear*).

B. These findings might be dismissed as merely interesting.

A. The situation becomes even more intriguing when we realize that Shakespeare was forty-six years old when the revision work was underway in 1610.

B. We shouldn't be surprised to find that Shakespeare played a role in translating this magnificently poetic portion of the King James Version.

One of the more intriguing literary legends surrounding the King James Version of the Bible alleges that Shakespeare's hand is present in the 46th Psalm. Turn to the psalm to see for yourself. Count to the forty-sixth word from the beginning of the psalm (*shake*) and then identify the forty-sixth word from the end of the psalm (*spear*). These findings might be dismissed as merely interesting coincidence. The situation becomes even more intriguing, however, when we realize that Shakespeare was forty-six years old when the revision was underway in 1610. We shouldn't be surprised to find that Shakespeare played a role in translating this magnificently poetic portion of the King James Version.

Chapter 24   Exercise D (p. 121)
Writing Varied Sentences

Giorgio Vasari, the Italian art historian who lived during the sixteenth century, records an interesting anecdote concerning Leonardo's use of models. For his models of the disciples, Leonardo drew from life, encountering difficulty only in locating a suitable Judas Iscariot. Throughout much of his work on the painting, Leonardo was troubled by the prior of Santa Maria, who monitored the work's progress from a vantage uncomfortably close for the artist. Upon hearing that the prior had expressed his concerns to Duke Sforza, Leonardo mentioned that any delay he had experienced was merely the result of his having encountered difficulty in identifying a model for the betrayer. But, Leonardo pointed out, he would be delayed no longer, for he had located his model: the prior would serve nicely.

Chapter 25   Exercise B (p. 123)
Writing Emphatic Sentences

When the European Vikings landed on a European coast, inhabitants learned to fear their sudden and fierce raids. These Norsemen sailed their high-powered boats from Scandinavia to the continent or Britain. They decorated their ships with striped sails and colorful circular shields. These ships brought little brightness to the raiders' victims. The Vikings left a permanent mark on the territories they attacked and occupied with ferocity and persistence. The Vikings' customs and language particularly influenced Norman France and the region of the British "Danelaw."

Chapter 26   Exercise B (p. 125)
Writing Concise Sentences

The seven daughters of Atlas, known as the Pleiades, were pursued by Orion, who was unable to seize any of them. Orion continued to follow them until Zeus took pity on them and placed them in the heavens. Although seven stars make up the Pleiades constellation, only six stars are clearly visible. The seventh is invisible except to those who have especially keen vision. In Greek mythology, the seventh star represented Electra, mother of Dardanus, who founded the Trojan race. The legend held that, rather than look down upon the destruction of Troy, Electra dropped from the sky. Today, though, with the aid of binoculars, well over seven stars are visible in this cluster. Viewing through a telescope yields several hundred.

Chapter 26 Exercise D (p. 127)
Writing Concise Sentences

Shakespeare's source for the story of *Macbeth* was Holinshed's *Chronicles*. There he found the account of King Duncan's murder, the suggestion about Lady Macbeth's ambition, and the tale of Macbeth's rise and fall.

Chapter 27 Exercise B (p. 129)
Using Parallelism

The location of the answers may vary.

1. a. Amy Rohling, one of the most talented people we know, is a painter, an actress, and a playwright.
   b. Amy Rohling, one of the most talented people we know, paints, acts, and writes plays.

2. a. The camera takes clear pictures and is easy to use.
   b. It is a camera that takes clear pictures and that is easy to use.

3 a. Megan Nelson manages to hold a responsible position, to earn an impressive salary, and to write a novel.
   b. Megan Nelson is holding a responsible position, earning an impressive salary, and writing a novel.

4. a. In the recording of popular music, the separate tasks necessary to produce, to arrange, and to engineer are often performed by one person who is called the producer.

b. In the recording of popular music, the separate tasks of producing, arranging, and engineering are often performed by one person who is called the producer.

5. a. When we are well rehearsed, when our timing is precise, and when our singer is in good voice, we sound as good as any other band in the city.

b. When we are well rehearsed, our timing is precise, and our singer is in good voice, we sound as good as any other band in the city.

6. a. On their first date, they were talking, eating, and drinking for hours after most others had left.

b. On their first date, they talked, ate, and drank for hours after most others had left.

7. a. Laura refuses either to go by bus or to ride the subway.

b. Laura refuses to go by bus or by subway.

8. a. Are marrying, child-rearing, and shopping all there is to life after graduate school?

b. Are to marry, to rear children, and to shop all there is to life after graduate school?

9. a. At thirteen months, my grandson Michael exhibits remarkable agility of movement, comprehends complex ideas, and shows aggressiveness of character.

b. At thirteen months, my grandson Michael exhibits remarkable agility of movement, comprehension of complex ideas, and aggressiveness of character.

Chapter 27   Exercise D (p. 131)
Using Parallelism

For hundreds and thousands of years, the Nile Valley experienced an annual flood. The Nile's floodwaters carried soil particles from upstream, deposited them throughout the flood plain, and renewed the fertility of the Egyptian fields. Although it might be interpreted as a natural disaster, the yearly event permitted the rise of one of the richest and most advanced ancient civilizations. The flood enabled the people to grow enough food to support a large population, allowing time for other activities, including building, scholarship, and art.

During the past century, construction of the Aswan High Dam has brought enormous changes to the Nile Valley. The dam is designed to retain an entire annual flow of the Nile and provide power to make cheap fertilizers, which are needed by the intensively cultivated farms that are no longer covered by silty Nile water. The dam has ended the Nile Valley's annual flood, which used to bring the region nutritious silt that was once cherished for its nutrients. Many people now consider the silt a nuisance because it fills up irrigation canals.

Review Exercise B for Chapters 24-27 (p. 134)
Composing Sentences

A Cliffhanger

Slowly I opened my eyes. As I looked to my right, I could see the huge rocks that lay awaiting a sacrifice fifty feet below. I looked to my left and could see the questioning faces peering over the edge of the cliff. Snowflakes fell gently around me. Suddenly I realized that only a flimsy gate stood between the boulders and me. I knew then that skiing was not the sport for me.

It all happened one day in January. I am still not sure why I had joined the school ski club, but it had seemed like a good opportunity to have fun and meet people. This was our first ski trip.

On the hour-long ride to the ski lodge, I wondered whether I would have been better off missing the trip altogether. I thought about everything that could possibly go wrong; I envisioned myself lying on a hospital bed with doctors standing all around trying to revive me. Although my friends had promised to teach me the basics of the sport, I could foresee a terrifying experience, and how right I was.

Yet when we reached the lodge. I rationalized the situation: This is skiing; it's supposed to fun. Feeling a bit courageous, I chose to begin on the intermediate slope. At the top of the mountain, when I looked down the icy terrain, visions of survival soon faded. With a few words of encouragement from a friend, however, I began to conquer the mountain piece by piece.

I skied about twenty feet at a time and then I stopped so I would not pick up too much momentum. This process continued with healthy results until I reached one particularly demanding part of the slope. It consisted of a sharp drop, followed by a ninety-degree turn. I was looking at a deathtrap waiting to engulf me. I said a quick prayer and pushed off, not knowing what lay ahead.

I handled the steep drop with minimal effort, but my luck ran out as I attempted to turn. I tried to maneuver around an unsuspecting skier and lost control. Instead of turning, I veered off the ski trail. Of course, I collided with the poor man and bent his ski poles, but this seemed trivial to me as I swiftly headed over the side of the cliff. In mid-air for a few seconds, I rushed head-on into a gate.

For a few seconds, I lay there in the snow, stunned, not realizing what had happened. Then, as I heard my friends calling my name and spectators asking if I were alive, I came back to reality. I had risked my life. I had been participating in something most people call a sport. Fortunately, only my pride was bruised, but I will never again slide down mountains on little pieces of wood.

Chapter 28   Exercise B (p. 137)
Choosing Words

Our neighborhood has many children. Every afternoon, the neighborhood children walk to the playground. If one child has a ball, all the children toss it around. If the swings are free, the Colton twins run over to them. Other children like the slide or the sandbox. Although each child has a favorite activity, most of them do nearly everything before it gets dark and they have to go home.

Chapter 29   Exercise B (p. 139)
Using a Dictionary

(Using *American Heritage Dictionary*, 3rd edition)

1. fast, faster, fastest
airy, airier, airiest
mere, no comparative, merest
homey, homier, homiest
unlucky, unluckier, unluckiest

2. bias: transitive, with no phrase
halt: transitive or intransitive, with no phrase
dissatisfy: transitive, with no phrase
turn: transitive, *turn a knob*;

intransitive, *wheels turning at a rapid rate*

Chapter 29 Exercise D (p. 141)
Using a Dictionary

(Using *American Heritage Dictionary*, 3rd edition)

1. a / maz / ing
amaz-ing
2. book / keep / er
book-keeper
3. cal / li / o / pe
calli-ope
4. lon / gi / tude
longi-tude
5. mark / ed / ly
markedly [no break]
6. mar / tyr
mar-tyr
7. side- / split / ting
side-splitting
8. thor / ough
thor-ough
9. tran / scen / den / tal / ism
tran-scendentalism or transcen-dentalism
10. un / like / ly
un-likely

Chapter 29 Exercise F (p. 143)
Using a Dictionary

(Using *American Heritage Dictionary*, 3rd edition)

1. **mountebank**: from Italian *monta im banco*, meaning "one gets up onto the bench"; refers to the bench stood on by hawkers of medicines at medieval fairs.
2. **pyrrhic**: if referring to metrical foot, from Greek *Purrikhos* inventor of a war dance; if referring to the victory, from King Pyrrhos, whose army defeated the Romans in 279 BC but was nearly destroyed itself.
3. **pittance**: from Old French term meaning allowance for food.

4. **protean** from Proteus, the Greek sea god who could change shape at will.
5. **fathom**: from Middle English *fathme*, meaning "outstretched arms."
6. **gossamer** from Middle English *gos* and *somer*, referring to the softness of goose feathers plucked in summertime.
7. **rigmarole**: from Middle English *ragmane rolle*, a scroll used in a Ragman, a game of chance.
8. **maudlin** corruption of Magdalene as in Mary Magdalene, who was often portrayed in Middle English literature as a weeping penitent.

Chapter 30   Exercise B (p. 145)
A Glossary of Usage

1. accept
2. effect
3. Whose
4. allusion
5. It's
6. your
7. their
8. among
9. complimented
10. conscious

Review Exercise B for Chapters 28-30 (p. 148)
Using Words Effectively

The following serves as one example of effective revision. (Pilot Mountain, North Carolina, may be better known as Mount Pilot, a town near Mayberry on "The Andy Griffith Show.")

Pilot Mountain

Towering above the foothills, enveloped in blankets of vibrant emerald pines and maples, lies my precious landmark, overshadowing the mere human creations at its giant feet. This colossus has a peculiar shape, as if God took His chisel and hand-carved each unique rock formation. Nowhere else on earth is there another such creation.

The best way to see the formation is from the second highest point on the mountain, known as the Little Pinnacle. To reach this spot, one must scale sharp, huge rocks; avoid steep, dangerous edges; and evade large, bulky trees. After the strenuous hike, one can rest upon any of the numerous, large rocks at the top of the Little Pinnacle and gaze upon the most famous point on the mountain: the Knob.

The Knob is perfectly rounded, with natural stone walls descending from its top. No vegetation grows on the walls. Thus, the tall pine trees rising from the top create an almost comical flattop hairstyle. On clear days, the Knob is visible from sixty miles away. From any point, it presents a remarkable sight, but the view from the Little Pinnacle is still the best.

Chapter 31   Exercise B (p. 151)
End Punctuation

1. Lochlin wondered whether he should take a nine o'clock class.
2. The instructor asked, "Was the Spanish-American War a victory for America?"
3. Are they really going to jump from that bridge?
4. Hoyt took a modest portion of dessert—half a pie.
5. "Is *data* the plural of *datum*?" he inquired.

Chapter 31   Exercise D (p. 153)
End Punctuation

Dr. Bertram Davis and his group of divers paused at the shore, staring respectfully at the enormous lake. Who could imagine what terrors lay beneath its surface? Which of them might not emerge alive from this adventure? Would it be Col. Jim Riser, chief scientist for the Royal Navy; Capt. John Fenstermaker, the director of security at the naval base; or Dr. Anne Rowe, author of numerous articles and books? Or would they all survive the task ahead. Dr. Davis decided some encouraging remarks were in order.

"Attention divers," he said in a loud, forceful voice. "May I please have your attention? The project that we are about to undertake—"

"Oh, no!" screamed Ms. Fox suddenly. "Look out! It's the Loch Ness Monster. "

"Quick!" shouted Dr. Davis. "Move away from the shore." But his warning came too late.

Chapter 32   Exercise B (p. 155)
The Comma

1. Monet, Renoir, Degas,
2. Angela, our most skillful speakers,
3. newspaper, gracefully
4. Slowly, slyly, and cautiously,
5. school, *It*, *Caesar*, *Juliet*,
7. that,
10. elephant, performer,

Chapter 32   Exercise D (p. 157)
The Comma

1. wand,	6. week,
2. Never, never	7. answer, wrong,
3. bacon, lettuce,	8. (no comma)
4. Who, opinion,	9. 18,
5. (no comma)	10. arrived,

Chapter 33   Exercise B (p. 159)
The Semicolon

1. Television soap operas provide a diversion to real life; their characters are often wealthy and never seem to work.
2. Ads on afternoon soap operas are directed primarily toward women and rarely at men; these ads for women include soap, toothpaste, skin creams, and nail products.

Chapter 33   Exercise D (p. 161)
The Semicolon

1. A good dictionary offers definitions of words, including some obsolete and nonstandard words; provides information about synonyms, usage, and word origins; and also offers information on pronunciation and syllabication.
2. Collecting baseball cards is a worthwhile hobby because it helps children learn how to bargain and trade; encourages them to assimilate, evaluate, and compare data about major league ball

players; and, perhaps most importantly, it encourages them to find role models in the athletes whose cards they collect.

Chapter 34   Exercise B (p. 163)
The Apostrophe

1. I'm, can't
2. child's, '76
3. bachelor's, country's
4. Y's, N's
5. Ooh's, ah's
6. hour's, day's
7. yes's, maybe's
8. ABC's
9. Cowarts'
10. Amy's, Jessica's
11. '77
12. partners'
13. She's, he's, children's
14. we'll, we're

Chapter 35   Exercise B (p. 165)
Quotation Marks

1. "Freedom of speech does not guarantee anyone the right to yell 'Fire!' in a crowded theater," she explained.
2. To many freshmen, "social security" means a date for Saturday night.
3. Wordsworth's phrase "splendour in the grass" was used as the title of a movie about young lovers.
4. *Beside* means "next to," but *besides* means "except."
5. "If everyone will sit down," the teacher announced "the exam will begin."

Chapter 36   Exercise B (p. 167)
Other Punctuation Marks

trouble;
discussed:
achievements;
games;
newspapers;

Chapter 36   Exercise D (p. 169)
Other Punctuation Marks

1. George Orwell's *1984* (1949) focuses on the dangers of a totalitarian society.
2. The final score (56-0) was a devastating blow for the Wildcats.
3. Hoyt told us that Belize (formerly British Honduras) offers spectacular off-shore diving opportunities.
4. The first phonics book (*Phonics Is Fun*) has a bright blue cover.
5. Some high school students participate in so many extracurricular activities (band, sports, drama club, and school newspaper, for instance) that they have little time to study.

Chapter 36   Exercise F (p. 171)
Other Punctuation Marks

1. *Checkmate*—a term derived from the Persian phrase meaning "the king is dead"—announces victory in chess. [Using parentheses is another option.]
2. The following people were present at the meeting: the president of the board of trustees, three trustees, and twenty reporters.
3. Before the introduction of the potato in Europe, the parsnip was a major source of carbohydrates—in fact, it was a dietary staple.
4. Liza Minnelli, the actress / singer who starred in several films, is the daughter of Judy Garland.

Review Exercise B for Chapters 31-36 (p. 173)
Understanding Punctuation

     Small towns and cities, especially older ones, face difficult financial problems. Their revenues are limited, but they're expected to maintain service levels, despite added costs. Sometimes the size of a town's annual budget is restricted by the state; in other cases, the local officials determine its size. Ultimately, such budgets are limited by the ability and willingness of citizens to pay the property taxes that generally fund such municipalities.

     When a municipal budget is strained, officials have two choices: increase revenues or cut expenditures. In the past, extra funds came from the state and federal governments, but now many towns must do without such aid. Instead, increased revenues can come only from new homes (whose owners pay property taxes), new or revitalized businesses (whose tax bills rise with their revenues), or new industry (whose taxes are a function of space occupied and revenues).

In an older town, however, with little vacant land, not much new growth can be encouraged. In addition, revitalizing an old, run-down business district requires time, capital, and community support. Thus, if revenues can't or don't grow, towns have no choice but to cut their expenses.

How can a town or small city spend less? One city manager summed up the problem when he said, "We're like a business during tough times. We have to be more efficient, more careful with our pennies, and more concerned about our customers—the demanding, overburdened taxpayers who depend on our services." And how does a town accomplish this? Few communities have long-term answers, for many fixed costs—pensions, utilities, insurance, and the like—are beyond their control.

Chapter 37   **Exercise B (p. 175)**
Spelling

1. accept
2. affected
3. capital
4. lie
5. there
6. exception
7. lose
8. license
9. Driving
10. already
11. possession
12. friendly

Chapter 38   **Exercise B (p. 177)**
Capitalization

1. fall, Angela, Erica, Beth, Brian, Halloween
2. Maple Street, highway, north, Cumberland State Park

3. Andrew Luke Thomas, Buddha, Buddhism, India
4. Americans, Roaring Twenties, Great Depression
5. George Elliot's *Middlemarch*
6. Mayflower Compact, Plymouth Colony
7. summer, Big Dipper

Chapter 39   Exercise B (p. 179)
Italics

1. schism
2. there, their
3. strombis pugilis
4. Los Angeles Times, Newsweek
5. Sixteenth Century Journal
6. Renaissance Studies
7. Mayflower
8. canteen, cantina
9. Ailuropoda melanoleuca
10. Messiah

Chapter 40   Exercise B (p. 181)
Hyphens

1. My pre-certification class has fifty-three students on the roster, but only thirty-seven have shown up.
2. By emphasizing her position as a middle-of-the-road independent, the little-known candidate hopes to win the runoff.
3. One of the restaurant's blue-plate specials is chicken-fried steak.
4. Both Texas and Virginia are right-to-work states.
5. Don stood on tiptoe to see the near-perfect statue, which was well-hidden by the security fence.
6. The new store in the mall has a self-service makeup counter and stocks many up-to-the-minute gadgets.
7. The so-called Saturday night special is opposed by pro-gun control groups.
8. For his pre-game meal, he ordered two all-beef patties with special sauce, lettuce, cheese, pickles, and onions on a sesame seed bun.

9. Although last night's speaker presented some thought-provoking insights, he hardly presented any earth-shattering conclusions.
10. The Braves-Mets game was rained out, so the long-suffering fans left for home.

Chapter 41   Exercise B (p. 183)
Abbreviations

1. St., throughout, February
2. eastern standard time, mountain standard time
3. Master of Arts, junior college, university, Tennessee
4. Introduction, Monday, Wednesday, and, Friday, Building
5. anthropology, literature, Christmas, afternoon

Chapter 42   Exercise B (p. 185)
Numbers

1. 12, 16-B, 75
2. June 8, 1985, $547
3. seven
4. 9 a.m. (or 9:00 a.m.)
5. 9, 22
6. Seventeenth, one o'clock, 6

Review Exercise B for Chapters 37-42 (p. 188)
Spelling and Mechanics

1. Although the calendar said January, it was a surprisingly warm, spring-like Thursday morning—January 28th, to be exact—and all Andrew could think about was how he would celebrate his birthday with his brothers.
2. Luke earned a four-year scholarship to the Florida public college of his choice; his goal is to earn an M.A. and then choose a graduate school where he can earn a doctorate.

3. One of the most famous of eighteenth-century literary pieces is Jonathan Swift's *Gulliver's Travels*, which we read in our English 218 class last semester.
4. The local teachers' union negotiated an excellent contract; each teacher will have twenty-seven paid holidays—including two weeks during the Christmas break; one week for the Easter break; and her birthday, plus the day before and the day after.

Appendix A   **Exercise B (p. 191)**
Parts of Speech

1. me
2. their
3. we
4. its
5. I
6. Who
7. Whom
8. Whom
9. I
10. me
11. us
12. He
13. me
14. she
15. me

Appendix A   **Exercise D (p. 193)**
Parts of Speech

1. The <u>doctor</u> is the <u>speaker</u> <u>who</u> will appear first.
2. <u>Our</u> cat lay on <u>my</u> <u>mother's</u> bed and licked the <u>boy's</u> chewing gum from <u>its</u> paw.
3. <u>Whom</u> did you invite to the party?
4. <u>We</u> will go there tomorrow.
5. The <u>governor's</u> speech astounded many members of <u>his</u> audience.
6. Give <u>it</u> to <u>them</u> or they'll complain to <u>me</u>.
7. <u>She</u> is as serious as <u>he</u>.
8. The police asked <u>whose</u> purse was missing.
9. The <u>brothers</u>, <u>Allen</u> and <u>Gene</u>, live in different states.
10. <u>His</u> swimming at noon is a daily ritual.
11. I sat behind <u>him</u> and <u>her</u>.
12. <u>His</u> coat is in <u>their</u> hall closet.
13. <u>Dr. Edmundson's</u> lectures are packed with interesting stories.
14. <u>They</u> can't walk far at this hour and in this weather.

Appendix A   **Exercise F (p. 195)**
Parts of Speech

1. C	6. I	11. I
2. I	7. C	12. C
3. C	8. I	13. I
4. I	9. I	14. C
5. C	10. I	15. I

Appendix A   **Exercise H (p. 197)**
Parts of Speech

1. curly	9. their
2. a	10. Both
3. tired	11. Each
4. sloppy	12. This
5. unsightly	13. These
6. lucky	14. tense
7. golden	15. a
8. sweet	

Appendix A   **Exercise J (p. 199)**
Parts of Speech

1. gently	9. slowly
2. carefully	10. fast
3. seldom	11. gracefully
4. perfectly	12. wildly
5. manfully	13. often
6. usually	14. more loudly
7. rarely	15. last
8. highly	

Appendix A   **Exercise L (p. 201)**
Parts of Speech

1. to	6. Between
2. in spite of	7. behind
3. across	8. among

4. above	9. toward
5. Before	10. before

Appendix A   **Exercise N (p. 203)**
Parts of Speech

1. During	6. with
2. On	7. of
3. at	8. into
4. against	9. In
5. under	10. On

Appendix A   **Exercise P (p. 205)**
Parts of Speech

1. Since	6. for example
2. and	7. or
3. While	8. nor
4. because	9. although
5. nevertheless	10. unless

Appendix A   **Exercise R (p. 207)**
Parts of Speech

1. Wow
2. Ouch
3. Oh
4. Heavens

Appendix B   **Exercise B (p. 209)**
Sentence Review

Answers will vary.

Appendix B   **Exercise D (p. 211)**
Sentence Review

1. s + v
2. s + v
3. s + v + sc

4. s + v
5. s + v + do
6. s + v + sc

Appendix C   Exercise B (p. 213)
Language Issues for International Students

Owned (past participle) is used as an adjective.
Owning (gerund) is used as a noun.
To own (infinitive) is used as a noun.
Rusting (present participle) is used as an adjective.
Rotting (present participle) is used as an adjective.
Staying (gerund) is used as a noun.
Moving (gerund) is used as a noun.
Ending (present participle(is used as an adjective.
Rolling (present participle) is used as an adjective.
Personalized (past participle) is used as an adjective.
Contained (past participle) is used as an adjective.

Appendix C   Exercise D (p. 215)
Language Issues for International Students

1. Because I transferred *many* credits from my *previous* school, I was
    able to graduate *early*.
2. *Too* often, *American* feminists feel they are describing the
    condition of *all* women in the world, when they are *actually*
    describing *only* women in America.
3. Kenjy *usually* works *many* hours on essays, but he remembers to
    take *periodic* breaks.
4. When you begin to exercise, start *slowly* and build *steadily* up to
    strenuous levels.